Wheelz

By
Steven C. Fotheringham

Published in America by WheelzBook

Copyright © 2015 by Steven Fotheringham

ISBN 978-0692413845
Ebook ISBN 06921413847
Book Cover design: Nathan Jaurez
Cover Photo by Marcelo Sayao[i]

Contents

Abandoned Baby.. 2

Pain... 19

Stair Rider... 22

Crutch Boy... 33

Preparation 39

Skate Park Guru.. 47

The Beginning... 57

Speed 70

Am Jam.. 79

WHEELZ.. 88

A Backflip 98

A Life of Its Own 107

Tour of Germany.. 118

Hardcore Sitting 125

Nike 132

A Handplant 134

ESPN Comes to Town 137

Stuntman 149

The X Games 163

A World Record..173

Leeder O. Men..178

The Speech 196

Unbreakable Chair 200

Nitro Circus..203

The Coach 211

Agent Mom 219

A Double Backflip 227

A Front Flip...233

MGM Grand 237

Life Rolls On 241

The MegaRamp 247

China Show 262

Rebel with a Cause 264

A Double Front Flip 274

WCMX 286

Down and Discouraged 304

Life Rolls On 2014 310

Conclusion 321

Abandoned Baby

Eight year old Ma Yibo sat in his wheelchair staring at kids on bikes and boards riding in wooden bowls the size of swimming pools. There inside of the huge warehouse, neither he nor his mother, who was by his side, could take their eyes off of the ramp that was higher than a house. Ma was sitting on wheels in a warehouse full of giant ramps. To him that was a bad combination. He started to look for an exit.

Ma rarely talked. Ma rarely did anything. He didn't attend public school and his parents basically kept him hidden. But Ma was the lucky one; at least his parents had kept him. Many parents in China, out of fear, lack of resources or embarrassment, give up children like Ma for adoption. Or worse.

But today was not a day to hide. Ma and his mother had come to Woodward of Beijing, a skateboarder's and BMX rider's paradise, by invitation -- better yet, by privilege. Still, they couldn't calm the fluttering in their stomachs and they couldn't fully ignore their urge to flee from this terrifying and unknown future.

That was when a pair of doors opened behind them and a crowd swarmed in: a parade of reporters, camera crews, fans, and supporters, all led by a young man on a bright green wheelchair.

The young man on the chair looked at the ramps like a skier who was starved for the slopes. He smiled a smile that any camera would love. He fastened his seat belt and pulled on its end as if he anticipated a rough flight. He strapped on a full-face helmet, his eyes focused on the highest ramp. Then, with no further pomp or prelude, he played.

The local riders were content to watch the show with the rest of the crowd. With the arms and shoulders of an iron worker he thrust his wheels up some ramps into a horseshoe shaped bowl. He shot up one side and then turned and used that speed to go up and out of the bowl on the other side. From there he rode to the top of that highest ramp.

Without any hesitation, the teen flew down that ramp and launched so high that he turned a slow motion backflip. It was like the world around him stopped for just a moment while he rotated. His face was content and calm.

For three seconds no one inhaled. Only index fingers on cameras moved. When he landed squarely on all four wheels, the crowd erupted.

He unstrapped his chair and let it slide to the bottom of the bowl. He pulled his lifeless legs up the steps back to the top of the ramp. Eager bikers rushed for the opportunity to bring up his chair. He strapped himself in and prepared for another trick. Ma was frozen.

When he hit the apex of his flight he thrust his arms forward as if he was trying to split a stump with an axe. This movement helped him to rotate through a front flip, landing in a foam pit.

But the young man wasn't finished yet. He returned to the horseshoe bowl. His eyes were bright and his smile contagious. He flew down that bowl with such force that he shot up the other side and went a couple of feet into the air This time he planted his hand on the coping as if to catch himself from going higher. The chair turned back towards the ramp and he tucked tight into a ball to miss the coping on his way down. As he reached the bottom, momentum shot him effortlessly back to the platform on the opposite side where he paused to rest for his next trick. He waited a minute to take it all in. It was obvious he had done these tricks thousands of times, but for all the onlookers everything was new.

The young man lifted three wheels and did a 360 spin on a back wheel. Then he plunged forcefully into another drop in. On the opposite side he rode the coping, two wheels floating in the air, as if he was riding sideways on a wall. Gravity beckoned him into the bowl where he finally came to a stop. Then he turned his attention to Ma Yibo.

He spoke through an interpreter, "Hi I'm Aaron. People call me Wheelz."

Ma said nothing. Aaron rolled over to Ma and brought his knuckles towards the little boy's clasped hands, smiled and said, "You'll be okay."

He strapped a helmet on Ma and grabbed the back of his chair. He gently pushed him up the ramps into the horseshoe bowl. The crowed followed in silence. Ma's mother stayed behind, frozen. .

Aaron guided Ma up and down and around the ramps. He showed him how to balance, how to shift his weight, what to look out for and what to wait for.
The boy's mother edged forward with eyes that were pasted on her son, her boy, being pushed into a new world. She snapped a few pictures on her phone. In less than fifteen minutes, Ma was on his own, pushing his wheelchair up and down small ramps. He was breathless, his arms ached, but a fire burned in his eyes.

His mother called her husband.
"You won't believe what our son is doing."

Wheelz

Five months later, Ma was attending public school on a new WCMX (WheelChair Moto-Cross) chair, jumping curbs, spinning, always on his two back wheels--his front wheels always up, jealous classmates looking on. He showed them videos of his hero from America.

He told his friends "I will one day be the Chinese Wheelz." Ma has a life -- a good one -- where he gets to ride and play. His parents have hope.

Ma could very well change a nation. He will need about ten years and a lot of practice, but the media will take notice. They will spread the word, and people will catch the fire. He will inspire more than those limited to wheelchairs. I know because I have seen it all before. Only the first time, it was my son.

I was there on that April morning in Beijing. I saw the change in Ma's eyes. Having witnessed so many similar miracles, I am uniquely qualified to tell this story. I was there from the beginning, mostly as an observer of a boy with an amazing attitude, but also an admirer of a mom who was behind him all the way. His story rightly begins with her.

Kaylene Fotheringham never says anything embarrassing in public because she never says anything in public. When we go out with friends, she is content to sit and listen. Our friends see the same poise and beauty I see. What they don't see is that behind her composed façade is a timid little girl.

Yet in spite of her shyness, when it comes to adopting children, she's like a lion after prey. Twenty-two years ago, I came home and was greeted by the lion.

"We need to talk," she said, pulling me into our bedroom and suggesting I sit down. I thought the worst: her sister, my brother, her mother--someone had died.

"There is a child in the hospital. We can have him if we want. There's just one problem. He has spina bifida."

"What's spina bifida?"

"It doesn't matter. It means he won't be able to walk." She looked at me intently. "We can't very well pray for another child and then, when we're offered one, turn him down because he has some problems."

"What are you doing praying for another child?"

She didn't answer, but her smile said, 'Too late. We're going after this one.' In this area I thought it wise to trust her instincts.

Wheelz

We met in May of 1978, at a dance held in one of the oldest church buildings in Las Vegas. It was built in the Tudor half-timber style, with a solid brick exterior and high, gabled roofs that looked as if they belonged somewhere in the Alps, not the heart of Sin City.

I came to Vegas to work a construction job, arriving only a week before that Friday night dance. I had just spent a couple of years in Australia. Returning home, I had a goal of dating twenty different Americans before I got serious with anyone. It was an odd goal. But I had my reasons.

Back then, my girl vibe radar was fairly good. I could tell the first girl I asked to dance was not into me. The second girl, though, there was something in her smile that could erode my 'twenty dates' goal. At the end of the evening, when the deejay announced a movie playing the next night, I made my way across the floor to ask her to go with me. I had no doubt that my invitation would be accepted.

Years later, she admitted having whispered to her friend, "Oh no! That dweeb is going to ask me to that movie."

I like my version better. The truth is she was too kind to tell me "no." We had fun at the movie and she laughed at my jokes. Evidently, she warmed to my dweeb ways because six months later we were married.

Wheelz

During our engagement the thought came to me, 'Kaylene needs to go to college with me.' Back then it was common for a wife to work to put her husband through college, so I thought the radical thought was inspired. However, Kaylene had no desire to get a degree. She wanted to be a mom. When I told her of my idea, she reluctantly agreed, with the provision that when she got pregnant, she would stop. Well, she didn't get pregnant and going to school, which she hated, merely added salt to her wounds. She graduated with honors, but her main ambition in life was beyond her reach.

We moved to Tucson Arizona where I began my teaching career. I loved teaching and I was pursuing other degrees. With a beautiful wife, a new apartment that included a pool, hot tub, and racquet ball court, I was happy. Kaylene was happy as well, except when she thought about the hole in her life. And that was only a couple of times a day. She cried a lot back then.

In November of 1984, after seven years of marriage, we adopted our first child, a beautiful girl with dark brown hair and eyes and we named her Lisa. Her mixed middle-eastern heritage gave her the most beautiful, light tan complexion. She was our Jordanian princess.

In October of 1987, when we adopted Brian I thought that was the end. The agency we got Lisa and Brian from only allowed for two adoptions per family. We would not be able to adopt more

Wheelz

unless we applied for a special needs child and we were not looking for challenges. I thought we were through: two great kids, no more tears. We moved back to Las Vegas and settled into our new home. Little did I know someone was praying behind my back.

Towards the end of 1991, a close friend called Kaylene, "I just heard that there's an abandoned baby you can have."

"What do you mean?"

"The child has spina bifida. His mother left him and didn't return. My doctor friend is sure she would consent to an adoption."

At Sahara Woman's Hospital the nurses were thrilled to have somebody visit the little baby. They led us to his crib where we saw this baby boy lying face down, his legs sprawled to his sides like a frog's. We were told this was a telltale sign of spina bifida. Kaylene picked him up and we saw a cute baby with dark brown hair and eyes with eyelashes that were and inch if they were a millimeter. As she embraced him I knew he would be ours. I wasn't too concerned about his not walking. This road called spina bifida didn't seem too daunting—cute kid, happy wife. But then again, on that evening, I couldn't see more than a few feet down that road.

We needed a little illumination, so Kaylene got a book on spina bifida. As we sat once more on the edge of our bed, she read to me. I listened, first with interest, then with a growing sense of dread. Her calm, clear voice narrated a catalogue of symptoms and complications, and I felt my initial intrigue grow cold. I lay back on the bed, my hands over my face, my insides growing nauseous. I was, to put it mildly, terrified.

According to what we read, our son would probably have weight problems because of a sedentary life. As a result, we would always need to have him on a strict diet. Though it seems counterintuitive, kids need to fall down a lot because that teaches them about consequences. If, because he couldn't walk, he missed that stage of development, he would most likely lack common sense. He would probably need many orthopedic operations, in addition to the bowel, bladder, and kidney problems that plague most kids with spina bifida.

He could suffer from neurological complications resulting in difficulty feeding and swallowing, breathing control and choking. It might even affect his upper arm function. He was at risk for hydrocephalus, which is an abnormal buildup of cerebrospinal fluid in and around the brain, and meningitis, a serious and sometimes deadly form of infection. He could have learning disabilities, allergies, skin problems, depression….the list seemed endless and the outlook was impossible.

I really did feel sick. I wondered if my new calling in life was to babysit a kid plagued with problems who would never have a life of his own. If so, I could accept it -- or, rather, I could resign myself to that fate -- but I really thought we were getting in over our heads.

I asked, "Are you sure you really want to do this?"

"I'm sure."

"Ok."

For some weird reason, if you intend to adopt a child in Nevada, the hospitals can't let you hold him or her until the adoption is finalized. A few weeks after we met baby Aaron he was taken to another hospital. He had contracted infant pneumonia (RSV).

Kaylene got a call, "Hi Mrs. Fotheringham, I'm Aaron's foster mom. He's at the University Medical Center. He's going to die if no one holds him. I lost another foster child, a little girl under similar circumstances, about a month ago. Aaron is getting cold and I honestly don't have the time he needs."

Kaylene hung up the phone, sped to the hospital, found where he was, and said, "Aaron's foster mother doesn't have the time to attend to him. I do."

She went to his room, picked him up, wrapped a blanket around him and sat in a chair next to his crib. No one stopped her. No one wanted to.

I went to see them that evening. "How's he doing?" I asked.

"Not good, he won't look at me." Her eyes were full of concern.

"You hungry?"

"Yeah, Chinese." I hurried out and returned with her dinner. She ate with one hand, never daring to put him down for a minute. For three days, when he was awake, he had a blank, distant stare.

We were told in one of our psychology classes that vivid contrasts, like a black and white checker board, tend to hold an infant's attention. When Kaylene was in high school her friends thought she ought to try out for the part of Snow White at Disney Land because of her light complexion and dark hair. So when Aaron finally looked up, he saw Snow White.

His blank gaze turned into a permanent, wide-eyed stare. He warmed up and he began to thrive. We knew from the start that he needed us, but now she needed him. By comparison to a natural birth their bonding process had been short. Nevertheless, they had a bond.

Wheelz

Our initial plan was to adopt him privately. As long as he remained a ward of the state, we didn't know what kind of care he would get and we didn't know how alone he would be. We did know, however, that agency/state adoptions take forever. In addition to the copious amounts of paperwork needed to meet legal requirements, we would also need FBI background checks, parenting training classes, CPR certification, home inspections, and more. We knew a private adoption would get him into our home faster. We just wanted to take him home.

I worked as a teacher at that steep, gabled building where I had first met Kaylene fourteen years earlier. Our lawyer, Tommy Deaver, drew up the paperwork and met me at my office in the basement of that building. He was ready to process the adoption, and I thought we were ready as well, but there was a huge roadblock that we couldn't see. If we went ahead as planned, the hospital could come back to us for medical expenses – and those expenses were enormous.

"Either option has its drawbacks," Tommy explained. "If you wait to go through the state and someone else requests a special needs child, you might not get him." After Kaylene's experience in the hospital, we couldn't consider that possibility. She was not going to let anything sever the connection that she had made with this little boy.

"But if you adopt him privately," he continued, "you may not be able to afford him. I suggest you let him fall to the state."

"But that could take forever" I said."

"Yeah but it won't bankrupt you."

As I walked him to the chapel door I said, "I'm going to need a few days on this one."

He reiterated, "I suggest you let him fall to the state. But if you want to go private, just sign those papers and drop that packet in the mail." We shook hands. He wished me luck and walked away. I walked back to my office.

Alone in the basement of a church is a good place to pray. I kneeled down with my forearms on my chair and said, "Heavenly Father, my lawyer says if we adopt this child privately it could cost us everything. I am willing to do that if that's what you want us to do."

I expected some kind of feeling...direction...answer. I got nothing.

I listened.

I waited.

Wheelz

Still nothing.

'This is a noble endeavor,' I thought. 'Surely it is God's will.' I needed an answer -- I thought I deserved one -- but nothing came to me.

I said, "If we let him go to the state there's a chance we won't get him and we're sure it will take a long time. We think that will hurt him. Please tell me which way to go."

No answer.

I thought, 'Give me a break. After all, this is a bit of a leap of faith.' I didn't say it out loud -- I didn't want to be disrespectful -- but it crossed my mind.

In the New Testament, James taught, "If any of you lack wisdom, let him ask of God, who giveth to all men liberally" (James 1:5). Well, I lacked wisdom, and I was asking. But all I got in return was frustration. So I stopped praying and I sat in my office and wondered.

I finally settled upon what I thought was a clever plan. If God truly wanted us to get this child, He would have to make it happen. If baby Aaron went to the state and someone else got

Wheelz

him, well, we had tried. Kaylene would be sad, but we could then assume it wasn't our destiny. Frankly, I would have been relieved.

I thought, 'If God's not going to give me an answer, I'm going to put the ball in his court. That meant letting Aaron fall to the state' I called Kaylene and she understood the decision. I could tell it was killing her to let him go.

I got on my knees again and said, "I feel like we should let Aaron go to the state. If he's to be ours please help us get him quickly."

As it turned out, the state didn't want to try to place a child with spina bifida, nor did they want to care for him until he was properly placed. There wasn't a long line of people looking for kids with disabilities, so they ignored all kinds of protocol. For one thing, we had already adopted two children, so they knew we would qualify eventually. Although the adoption process would take months to complete, we brought Aaron home within a couple of weeks. We saw it as a miracle. (Anyone who has tried to adopt a child or register their car with a government agency knows what I mean).

We also learned that since Aaron was a ward of the state they would pay all of his future medical bills. That little piece of information would have made our decision much easier.

As I look back at the miraculous parting of the bureaucratic red tape and the dozens of operations we never could have afforded, I see things more clearly. I did get an answer after all. "Put the ball in my court. I'll take care of it." I asked, I received. Aaron was ours.

This book is not about religion even though our beliefs have everything to do with this story. We believe there is more to our existence than this life. If we didn't believe that, then there is no way we would have adopted Aaron. We believe we are saved through faith in Christ. Faith to us means we trust Him. Because of that belief, when He says "jump," we jump. We truly felt we were supposed to adopt Aaron. And so we jumped.

But I was still afraid. I thought that I would spend my life carting this kid around. I imagined him on the sidelines of every sport, other kids staring at him there I'd be, trying to explain why he was different. My thoughts were dark. Sometimes, at night, when he was a baby, I would hold him and sway to the music of The Phantom of The Opera. "No more talk of darkness / Forget these wide-eyed fears / I'm here – nothing can harm you / My words will warm and calm you." [ii]

I know it sounds sentimental, but these words defined my job as Aaron's protector dad. I was resigned to my role. I believed that song would be my inspiration. I could not have been more wrong.

Wheelz

Pain

"He's their hero. He's their champion. And he's teaching them that there are no limits when you have the heart of a champion." Diane Sawyer (2/13/2008, *ABC News, Good Morning America*).

As I said, Kaylene and I couldn't have children on our own. Well-meaning friends tried to console us with comments like, "You know, there are advantages of not having children." Such comments never helped.

After years of heartbreak and frustration, a day came when my dad asked, "So what's the problem?" It was his kind way of seeking understanding. We explained. His answer was like cool water to our thirsty souls. "It must be hard."

We found an unexpected comfort in his acknowledging our situation and letting us own our pain. We didn't need consolation; we needed understanding. And that simple line fit the bill. When you meet someone who has a child with spina bifida, try that line.

Spina bifida is a neural tube defect that usually happens during the first trimester of pregnancy. Part of the lower vertebrae do not form properly, so in the worst cases, a portion of the spinal cord develops outside the protection of the backbone, resulting in,

Wheelz

among other things, impaired function in the lower limbs that can range from simple loss of sensation to complete paralysis. The subsequent complications often include club foot or feet, hip dislocation, scoliosis and a tethered cord, among other things.

Aaron suffered from almost all of these complications, and his history of surgeries and hospitalizations was long and painful. Before he was a year old he had undergone three major surgeries. In addition, he had the infant pneumonia I mentioned earlier. At five months old Aaron went in for a club foot repair and came out with his Achilles tendon cut. I was livid.

"Why would you do that?" My wife asked an orthopedic surgeon whose clinical acumen and surgical skills far outclassed his bedside manner.

"It's technical. I'll explain it to your husband when he gets here," he said.

She was hit with a wave of shock and unbelief that a man could be so condescending to a woman in the 1990's. She took a step back. She was unprepared for a response. But all of that was eclipsed by her concern about the outcome of the surgery.

His Achilles tendon was cut. She called me.

I hurried down to his office and asked the same question. "Now there's no hope of him ever walking. Why would you take that away from him?"

He gave us no medical explanation. "This is standard care for infants with spina bifida."

"Why is it standard care?" I asked.

"It just is."

This is the answer you didn't think my wife would understand? I thought. I'm sure he knew I was upset, but he had no clue how much I was holding back. I was furious. I wanted to scream with rage, but I remained calm in an effort to coax the reason out of him. It didn't help. He had nothing to give us.

Up until that moment, I'd thought there was a possibility Aaron might walk. Some children with spina bifida can, with crutches or with the help of a walker, or even on their own sometimes. Without his Achilles tendon, Aaron would never have a chance.

I called my friend, Doctor Steve Thomas, a brilliant orthopedic surgeon.

I said, "I know you're booked for weeks but I've got to see you today. There's no way I'll be able to sleep until we get some answers."

He responded, "Get down here as quickly as you can." We drove straight to his office.

"He did the right thing," Steve explained calmly after hearing our experience. "The cut actually adds stability. His muscles won't fight against him. It's a common procedure, fully supported by the literature and by clinical evidence."

His explanation assuaged our anger, but any shred of hope that he might walk was annihilated. We drove away from his office in silence.

While we prepared for the worst, Aaron went about the business of growing up, completely unaware of and unconcerned by our worries. If anything, our baby was thrilled to get that cast off his leg. So while we waded through fears and ominous thoughts of the future he was moving on; on his own and in his own way.

Stair Rider

Aaron learned to crawl at the same time as other kids his age. Because of his paralysis he couldn't take advantage of his leg muscles but that didn't slow him down. He navigated the rooms in our house by pulling himself across the floor with his arms. Like any other baby, he went wherever he wanted to go. He covered so much ground on our tile floors, dragging his legs behind him. This earned him the nickname "Mop." His pajamas were always filthy but our floors sparkled.

At the age of eleven months Aaron learned to go down stairs. Head first.

He slid up to them on his belly and then leaned forward until gravity worked in his favor, each hand catching the next step.

Note: There are nine short videos that accompany this book. Readers who watch them as they come up will have a great experience with this biography. A PDF that accompanies the audiobook contains those video links. Also pictures and video links can be found at Wheelzbook.com. Download a QR Reader app! They're free and when you activate your reader and point your device at the code below, you can watch the video for free!

VIDEO 1: This video documents one of Aaron's early attempts on stairs.

http://youtu.be/7LlHbNhp5h8

The staircase to our basement was split in two with five stairs that led to a landing followed by six more stairs to the bottom floor. It wasn't long before it took only a few seconds for Aaron to complete the whole flight. It was only the turn of the stairs that slowed him down. So one day we took him to a model home that had a long straight run of stairs.

I positioned him at the top of the stairs, and said "Wait 'till I say 'go.'"

I ran down to the bottom and said "GO!"

Aaron flew down those stairs like a seal on a wet slide. His hands were keeping him on course, pounding each step in a blur. Kaylene and I cheered. I picked him up and took him up for another run.

He was in the middle of a run when a lady opened the front door. She saw him and screamed.

Wheelz

I said, "No, no, he's ok. He loves going down stairs that way." She looked at us as if we were crazy, turned and left. We didn't care! Our boy was having a blast.

Aaron was full of life and ambition. Early on we knew that he had a good sense of humor. He was lying on the couch once -- he couldn't have been older than three -- flat on his back and I leaned over and said something like, "You're a cute kid."

He stared at me for a moment, lost in serious contemplation, and then, as though he had been hit with sudden inspiration, said, "You only have one eyebrow!"

"Funny kid," I said.

To our surprise, Aaron learned to walk with a little walker. That didn't last long. At about three, he graduated to crutches. He had no problem using both. He liked his walker but he loved his crutches. They soon became a toy that he played with. He swung in midair on them and pretended they were guns and shot people with them. He put decals on them.

At church, Aaron walked through the halls to choruses of "Oh, how cute," and "Isn't he adorable!"

Those who vocalized such sentiments were usually rewarded with a sharp smack in the shins from a hard, metal crutch. (He didn't much like being called cute.) It was convenient, though, having the boy with the crutches. I could always find him in those crowded halls by looking for the person doubled over, rubbing his shins.

By age five, he could walk on his hands, upside down, as far as he wanted. He worked hard at going up and down stairs with his legs in the air and when he wanted to work harder, he had me take him to the park to practice on stairs. It garnered a lot of attention from passersby who stopped to watch.

When he was old enough to write, he wrote:

"I'm good at walking on my hands. It is very fun. I can do tricks like jumping up and down, push-ups, going in reverse, running, walking off stuff, and standing on one hand.

You have to be careful not to fall. Once you get used to doing it, you will love it. It takes lots of practice. If you eat a lot, you can't do it. I have been walking on my hands since I was four years old.

Walking on your hands can be dangerous sometimes. For example, you could fall and hurt your head. Once I fell and it didn't hurt. Well, most of the time it doesn't hurt. Once I walked off a big box onto a small box and off the small box onto the ground.

It is the funnest talent I have ever done. I love it to death. It's my best hobby. It's wonderful. Also it is a good exercise. You should try!"

Aaron was walking on his hands and with the help of crutches, his feet. But he still needed medical attention. After the Achilles tendon incident, Kaylene researched other options for his medical care. When we ended up at Primary Children's Hospital in Salt Lake City, UT, we knew we had found the right place.

I'm sure there are hospital staffs in Las Vegas that really care for their patients. We just never found one that worked for us. There was a kind nurse or two. But more times than not, we encountered bureaucratic protocol more than patient care. The nurses barged into the room in the middle of the night to wake my son up to check his vitals. We honestly figured they were bound by some law because no one and no institution of healing could be so thoughtless.

At Primary Children's Hospital, we learned there is no such law. If one of their patients was sleeping, they would actually postpone their routine vitals checks until he woke up! They had this radical belief that sleep is an important component in the healing process.

Wheelz

That alone was an astounding difference, but it wasn't the only one.

None of the Las Vegas hospitals wanted his mother to sleep in his room while Aaron was post-operative. At best she was given a chair. Primary Children's brought in a bed and made it up for her, close to his so she could be by his side.

And at Primary Children's we met Dr. Smith, whose wealth of experience in treating children with spina bifida, coupled with his friendly and reassuring manner, sealed the deal for us. It was Dr. Smith who recommended Aaron get his first wheelchair when he was only three years old.

I was totally against it. He was walking fine with braces on his ankles and crutches. I wanted him to stay with crutches. That book we had read -- the nausea-inducing one — was always in the back of my mind. I figured it would be good for Aaron to always fight to stay on his feet.

"That's fine, Dad," Dr. Smith said. "But if you wait until Aaron has to use a chair, he'll feel like a failure. Just get him one as an option. Then, if he ever needs it, the transition will be easy."

We got him a chair. In the beginning, Kaylene took him to the recreation room in our church building and let him chase his brother and sister in his chair on a smooth floor. He liked being able to keep up with them -- to catch them sometimes.

When you use your arms as legs they become as strong as legs. By the time Aaron was four, he had arms that were stronger than any kid twice his age. Kaylene had to enlist Lisa's and Brian's help holding him down so she could administer his daily medication. It was painful and tasted awful, and he was too young to understand why he needed it, so he fought the three of them daily for the longest time.

The surgeries, however, were worse. Spinal column surgeries, club foot repairs, Achilles tendon -- it seemed endless. Walking on his hands, walking with crutches and navigating in a wheelchair all tested his physical strength, but surgery tested a different kind of strength altogether.

As a testament to the superior care of Primary Children's Hospital, Kaylene and Aaron made the eight-hour (one-way) trip at least twice a year during the first decade of his life, generally during record-breaking snowstorms.

I think I was as supportive as any father could have been, but one operation in particular broke me. It was called a bilateral osteotomy. The muscles in Aaron's legs had atrophied and this resulted in his hips continually dislocating. Dr. Smith suggested the radical surgery. It required basically cutting his femurs – the

Wheelz

largest leg bones – in half, then reattaching them at an angle so that his legs would turn in toward his hips.

When my wife described what needed to be done, I folded. I had never before nor since shut down because of some problem, but the thought of my little boy's legs being cut in half was more than I could stand.

"I'm sorry," I said. "Please don't talk to me about this again. Just do it. Don't describe it."

Kaylene had always been the one to take care of Aaron during his operations but she usually shared the minutest details with me. This one had to be different. She could talk about everything I needed to handle at home and about her arrangements in Salt Lake, but as far as describing the horrors of the surgery, she kept silent. I don't know to what degree that added to her burden. It was too much for me to consider. I imagine it was worse on her because she was absorbed in the details. And yet she went forward, this time alone.

Dr. Smith said the operation went well, but Aaron lost a lot of blood. He was pale. Usually after an operation, he would wake up in a matter of hours. This time he was out for three days.

The doctors also worried about the edema in his ankles and feet. They were far too swollen. They talked seriously about cutting off the cast and waiting for the swelling to go down.

One thing I love about Kaylene is her pessimism. She's always sure that we'll be late or there won't be any parking or the light will turn red before we get to the intersection. I love it because she's almost always wrong, so she lives a life of unexpected positive surprises.

With Aaron out for days and her tendency to expect the worst, Kaylene was frantic. She didn't sleep at all and she refused to leave his side. All that she did the entire time was worry.
Then, on the afternoon of the third day, he woke up. The first thing he saw was Kaylene. She gently brushed his hair off his face and whispered "How you feeling?"

He spoke four words that told her all was well, "I want a hamburger."

Twenty-four hours later they headed for home with Aaron in a full 'spika' cast.

The cast went from under his ribcage to his ankles. There was a rod in between his legs to keep them stationary. Until the cast came off, we had to carry him everywhere.

This surgery took Aaron to the depths of despair. He was only five years old, dealing with the pain of a grown man and stuck in a body cast that kept him from doing anything. For a kid as active as Aaron, it was sheer torture. He was frustrated and angry. He hit anything that came within range and broke anything within reach. Kaylene went with him to anger therapy for several years while he learned coping strategies; it was a difficult time for all of us.

But pain such as Aaron's can also excavate the soul, making room for among other things, empathy. This surgery hadn't been Aaron's first, nor would it be his last, but in spite of what he still has to learn, in spite of what he didn't and doesn't understand, no one can relate better than him. When he visits kids in different hospitals, he knows how they feel. He laughs with them. He's comfortable with them because he is one of them. And that can make a world of difference.

Crutch Boy

It was an unusually quiet moment in our white Nissan van when six-year-old Aaron broke the silence: "I make this my rule: I don't kiss dead people."

My grandmother's funeral had been a few weeks before, and Aaron must have seen someone kiss her and decided such things were not for him.

"Good rule!" My wife and I said together. "Family rule."

Aaron was born into a world of rules he didn't agree with. Most of the world, including his parents, saw wheelchairs as confining. He didn't agree. One time, someone made a suggestion that he wear a full face helmet when small helmets were the fad. He thought it through and made that suggestion his rule. His teachers insisted all four wheels stay on the ground. That was a rule he couldn't follow. If someone called him a cripple that was fine because, in his book, cripples were cool.

It was interesting (to say the least) to see him blaze a path hundreds would follow. As we watched him grow we would often turn to each other, smile, and say, "Good rule."

In 1985, seven years before Aaron was born, an artist named John Lytle created a comic strip entitled *Leeder O. Men*, about a young man who did amazing stunts at skate parks in a wheelchair. When

Wheelz

we met John years later, he would say, "I've waited for Leeder O. Men to come. He has and his name is Aaron."

For years, any suggestion from me that he was a role model or some kind of influence really bothered my son. In his mind he was, pure and simple, a kid who loved playing at the skate park.

When he got his crutches you would have thought that he'd gotten a new bike. He saw them as toys. His playing at the skate park was merely an extension of an attitude he had early on. The more he played, the more people were attracted to him. When Aaron was about seven years old he wrote a book about a superhero he named "Crutch Boy." He made Crutch Boy a little older (eleven) to give him respectability.

Getting to Know Crutch Boy

"Hi, I'm Crutch Boy. I'm eleven years old. I have freaky powers. I figured out that I had them when I was five. I was in kindergarten and I got pushed down by a kid and I got mad and well I was thinking how cool it would be if my crutch flew out of my hand and hit him.

You know that people say, 'Be careful what you wish for.' Well, I should have. It flew out of my hand and hit the kid. Boy, was I in trouble that week. I had to figure out that my crutches were magic the hard way.

Wheelz

It was neat to know I had magic crutches. I wanted more proof they were magic. So I rubbed my crutches and said, 'I wish you crutches would hit me in the head!'

Big mistake! They were magic. So as you might have guessed, they hit me in the head hard! So now I'm having fun with my crutches (drawn squiggly like he's dizzy).

I also have a new friend Wheelchair Boy."

I'd voiced my reservations about getting Aaron a wheelchair when he was a toddler, but he realized none of my fears. His wheelchair, like his crutches, was always a toy. By second or third grade, he was alternating between crutches and his chair, and when he wrote about them, he always included dollar amounts. I think to his young mind, high costs meant they had true value.

My Wheelchair, Crutches

"I have a wheelchair. It cost 2,500 dollars. It is for hospitals, but I use it for jumps. It is not good for it so I'm getting a new one. It'll be a sporty one.

I also like my crutches. They cost 200 dollars each. I can do tricks with them. I put my feet up and I walk with the crutches. If you take the crutch tips off, black oil comes out. Crutches last for years.

Wheelz

I also have a walker. I think it cost about 300 or 400 dollars. It won't go backwards so you won't fall down. I can also do tricks with it. It has red handles. I like it!!!

The End"

Another Entry

"I'm getting new crutches and a new wheelchair. My wheelchair will be midnight blue. So will my crutches. I got to choose the color. I should get it before February is over. The wheels will be tilted so it can turn easy. There will not be any handles so people can't push me. I'm so excited. I'm also excited about getting my crutches. The ones I wear now are two hundred dollars for each one."

And so for Aaron a rule that permeates every fiber of his being is the attitude he had from the beginning: I'm lucky to be crippled. At times that was challenged. There were naysayers. But he would hear none of it.

We were swimming at my friend's house. He and Aaron were playing in the pool. Aaron got too intense and kept splashing my friend when he should have stopped. The next thing I knew my friend said, "Stop it, you gimp."

Aaron stopped. I figured he was hurt. *I* was hurt. I pulled my friend aside and told him that was inappropriate. But Aaron was going to have to deal with situations like this on his own. We always knew he had to.

Weeks later Aaron was working on a project in my wife's sewing room. When he came out we saw he had made a little sign on white cloth. It was about nine inches wide and six inches high and said, "Gimps Rule." He asked his mom for safety pins to pin his sign on the back of his chair. With that he was off to school.

His friends thought it was cool. We thought it was cool. But his teacher called with deep concerns.

"He's dealing well with his disability," Kaylene explained. "Let it go."

The teacher couldn't let it go. The sign came off, but the attitude did not.

Around the same time, Aaron started attending a summer camp for children with special needs promoted by Primary Children's Hospital. He liked getting away from home, enjoyed the outdoor activities, and loved the counselors. Every year he came home saying the same thing: "To see some of those kids' challenges makes me appreciate how well off I am."

Wheelz

He went for two or three years but eventually stopped because the staff kept treating him like he was disabled. They would tell him he couldn't ride down stairs or do some of the "wild" things he did. I'm sure he did what he did for attention, but even back then he knew he had a message to share. He did that by merely playing. But he also had something to say. The camp had a talent show. For his talent at his first camp he wrote a poem. It began, "All my friends think I am hipida because I've got spina bifida."

The day would come when organizers of such camps would beg for Aaron to come and demonstrate what he was once asked not to do. They would fly him to their camps and cover his expenses for him to share with their youth the message "Gimps rule."

His disability came with more operations. As they increased in number, he seemed to wear the number as a badge of honor. He was seven years old when he went in for surgery to have steel pins put in his ankles. It was the second attempt to increase stability in his lower limbs. It hurt as usual. But Aaron liked the times when it was just he and his mom alone.

Those times, which would be many, would become more precious because Kaylene had her eyes on two more children.

Preparation

Kaylene and I were sitting in a teacher's symposium in Provo, Utah. The speaker, who was exceptionally inspiring, was talking about going after lost sheep. When he finished, Kaylene said, "We're going to adopt a little girl out of Moldova."

I protested, but I didn't have a chance.

Her exact words were "You'll get used to the idea."

A dozen thoughts flooded my mind. *We can't afford this. That guy's talk had nothing to do with adopting kids. How does she know of such a place? She must have been researching this for a while.*

After about two months of watching her frantically doing all the paperwork, I caught her looking on the computer at pictures of kids in the orphanage. The weird thing was the pictures she was looking at were of boys.

She said, "Oh, by the way, we're getting a little boy while we're at it."

Now I was concerned even more about costs. One kid cost about twenty-five thousand dollars. Another kid . . . well, the math isn't difficult.

Wheelz

She told me not to worry about the money. "You'll get used to the idea." Then she added, "We need the little girl. The little boy needs us." That turned out to be prophetic.

Her trips to Moldova were each a story of their own. Suffice it to say, within the year we had two more children.

The girl's name was Christina. No one knew who she was or where she was from. She had been abandoned next to a fencepost. We liked her name, so we didn't change it but we did get to choose her birthdate. She was a beautiful baby and is a beautiful girl.

The little boy's name was Yuri. We named him Michael Yuri.
The director of the orphanage couldn't understand why we wanted him. He told us "The child will be an outlaw."

Mikey had a club foot, a defect that seemed to embarrass the orphanage officials. We could tell from the way his chin seemed glued to his chest that he had been neglected. We felt his coming to our home was inspired because we knew much about club feet and we knew the perfect doctor and hospital to solve that problem. What we didn't know was that he was also mentally and emotionally disabled.

Mikey, to put it mildly, was a nightmare. He couldn't talk and wouldn't go to bed. He wanted constant attention and would do

Wheelz

anything to get it. When he wanted something, he screeched, so when we locked him in his room to get him to go to sleep, our home sounded like a haunted house. He was completely lovable if you played with him, but if you left him in a room alone it would be flooded or the T.V. would be crashed to the floor.

Years after Mikey could walk, I heard a pitter-patter up on the roof.

That's weird,' I thought. *'It's not even Christmas.*

I found Kaylene in our bedroom. "Where's Mikey?" she asked.

At that moment two thoughts dawned on me: one, I don't believe in flying reindeer, and two, that sound on the roof was Mikey. I got Mikey safely down, although he thought it hilarious that I had to catch him on the roof, and then proceeded to chop down the tree he had used as a ladder.

As Kaylene had predicted, he did indeed need us. When people learned of our situation, they almost always said, "You've got your hands full."

We always said, "Yeah."

During the year of those adoptions, Kaylene made three successive trips to Moldova in addition to the trips she made to

Primary Children's Hospital for Aaron's surgeries and follow-up appointments. Any time a surgery required placing hardware inside of his body, it called for a second surgery to remove that hardware. It ran Kaylene ragged. But for the boy who could find advantages in a walker, there were things about those trips he loved; most importantly, he had his mom to himself.

We had five children, one of whom was Mikey, and I sometimes wondered if we would make it out of their collective childhood in one piece. In spite of it all, Aaron thrived. He endured the surgeries and turned the comments of the naysayers on their heads. He was going places, and nothing and nobody was going to stop him.

One of the first obstacles that Aaron faced was tip casters. Tip casters are rods that extend out of the rear of a wheelchair with little wheels on their end. They are designed to keep kids from tipping their chair over backwards and hitting their head. At three, Aaron had me remove those things; another rule was "Tip casters must go."

He practiced getting his chair's front wheels off the ground all of the time. If he was watching TV or doing homework, he was almost always on just two wheels. In school, his teachers got upset because he wouldn't keep all four wheels on the ground. By junior high, he usually sat on just one wheel, leaning on his desk, because that was more comfortable.

His teachers were rightfully concerned for his safety. We wrote letters assuring them that leaning on one wheel was necessary for his back. It took me a long time to realize the benefit of treating his chair like a two-wheeler. On rough, rocky terrain, those little front wheels could do more harm than good. They got caught on rocks and obstacles in his path and threatened to tip him over. They slowed him down. But with the front wheels up, Aaron could go anywhere, up sidewalk curbs and even stairs, a difficult feat made possible only by balancing on the back two wheels.

I don't know how long it took him to learn to jump a curb, nor do I recall him practicing it. We were walking towards a store one day when Aaron suddenly flew right at the curb with his front wheels in the air. He hit the curb with his rear wheels hard enough to bounce the chair into the air, and his momentum carried him forward onto the sidewalk.

Years later, I videotaped him at a skate park.

"Get this," he said, then lifted his front wheels in the air, put his back wheels at the face of a step, pushed against it with a slight hop, and rolled upward. He flew up those twenty stairs in almost no time at all.

I thought, '*If he falls backwards, he's dead.*' But he went up and down with ease, his front wheels rarely touching anything.

Wheelz

Aaron always liked who he was. I remember driving up to a handicap parking spot and hearing him say, "I like it: they always have a picture of me."

He had claimed that symbol for himself. He drew it constantly, though he added a helmet and tilted it backwards on two wheels. That would one day become his logo.

One time he drew the little handicap symbol breaking out of a sign. He was floating halfway down with a parachute. He had made the handicapped sign into his own personal Bat Signal.

Aaron's journal entries from fourth grade showcase his attitude.

> September/22/2000, I'm going to get a new wheelchair. I hope it will have my favorite colors, red and black. It will be a sport wheelchair. It will go fast!
>
> October/11/2000, A lot of people ask me what happened? Now I say nothing's wrong with me, what happened to you? I only say that sometimes. If the kid keeps on asking I say that. They always want a ride in my wheelchair. I say no way, José! My dad won't let you.
>
> October/17/2000, I have had eleven operations, one or two every year. But I don't think I need them anymore. I go to Salt Lake, Utah, for them. There is a very nice doctor there. His name is Dr. Smith. He is the best. He

does the operation on me. When he's done operating I go to the cafeteria to eat. Sometimes I throw up. He gives me stuff like socks to put on before he operates on me. He puts me on a medicine called Anotheza. I can choose the flavors: bubblegum, root beer, mint, cinnamon. The root beer doesn't smell good at all. The car trip takes eight whole hours to get there. There is a doctor that is going to order me a new wheelchair. I hope I can choose the colors on it. It's going to be a sporty wheelchair with big wheels. It will go very, very, very fast. It will be neat.

If the teacher liked his daily entry, she stamped that page "Great Work." At the end of that last entry, Aaron wrote "Stamp here." That time, his teacher gave him a huge red star.

Having his front wheels up was more than a trick for getting up stairs. It was pivotal for Aaron's future career and a perfect indicator of his attitude about the chair and his abilities. For example, when his high school spotlighted him during a pep rally in the gym, they screened one of his short videos and then called for him to come to the flat gym floor. He entered from the top of the bleachers, bouncing down the twenty or so huge steps, one step at a time, front wheels always in the air. Bang! Bang! Bang! The wooden steps echoed throughout the gym as he dropped and paused on each of them. Later on, as a guest on a kids' game show in Germany, he made the same entrance.

President Lincoln was once asked how he was able to become the President of the United States.

His answer was "I kept preparing myself just in case." [iii]

Although Aaron never voiced that thought, it is exactly what he did. When he had us remove those tip casters, there were no skate parks in Las Vegas. He didn't know how dramatically his future would collide with those parks a few years later, but he prepared every day as though he did. As he practiced, giant earth movers and hundreds of concrete trucks and large construction companies began to roll.

Skate Park Guru

Sometimes it seemed as though the universe was orchestrating the entire plot of Aaron's life. At the very least, every thing he needed entered at the perfect moment. Aaron had the skills, the determination, and the attitude, but he also happened to be in exactly the right place at exactly the right time. When he was ready to ride skate parks, we lived within easy rolling distance of four of them. Those parks hadn't been there a few years earlier, and the competitions that became his mainstay wouldn't be there a few years later. They were the blood, sweat, and toil of a man who spent his young adult life in pursuit of a dream, a man named Joe Wichert.

Joe grew up in California in the 1970s. He loved skateboarding and riding BMX and spent most of his youth at the Del Mar Skate Ranch in San Diego, where Tony Hawk took skateboarding to a whole new level. He knew Tony; he saw him there all the time. During the first half of that decade, skate parks popped up all over the state. But society's apprehensions shut them down just as quickly, alienating an entire group of athletes and turning skateboarders and BMX riders into outlaws.

When Joe was fourteen, he moved with his family to Las Vegas. Riding was still his consuming passion, but there were few, if any, skate parks in town. He ground every handrail. He jumped every flight of stairs. He made and jumped his own ramps. When he thought about his future, riding was all he could think of.

"You're wasting your time with this," his dad said. "You're going nowhere."

His mom would chime in, "You need to buckle down and go to college."

Joe wanted no part of it.

He wasn't a bad kid and he never gave his parents any trouble. He just wanted to ride. He was blind to any other options. He ditched school to hang out at the Mirabilli Community Center, volunteering to help with the most menial tasks.

The staff told him, "Joe, you can't be here. You're supposed to be at school." But he wouldn't go away.

He had his bike and skateboard and a little motorcycle. He'd ride to the center, work out in the gym, and volunteer. He fixed things and swept up. Finally he was offered a job -- just a little one, at first. But that little job turned into other little jobs. He had a dream that became an obsession to bring skate parks to Las Vegas, and he saw even the smallest job as a foot -- or maybe a toe -- in the door.

Wheelz

Joe's first chance to wedge that door open came when he learned of a posting for a Junior Recreation Leader. It was an entry-level, full-time position, and the competition was stiff. Vegas was booming; the Parks and Recreation Department was stuffed with people who had college degrees, people who were interning with the city in the hopes of getting that job.

Joe was barely eighteen and employed only part-time at the rec center. He was outeducated and outnumbered, but he saw the position as the next step toward reaching his goal. So he spent his time studying for the Junior Recreation Leader test.

"Give me every recreation book you guys have," he told his bosses.

Joe turned into a bookworm overnight. The test was difficult. The good thing was that the information was fresh in his mind whereas the other applicants had to remember things they had studied four years earlier. He assumed that was why he was the only one who passed the test.

The staff at the Human Resources department was flummoxed. They couldn't believe that Joe, with the least amount of experience and education, was the only one who had passed their test. They accused him of cheating.

"We're going to retest you for this position," they said.

Wheelz

But Joe knew the rules "No, that's not what it says. If I passed your test and I'm the only one who did you've got to hire me. I'm not falling for this."

They conceded his point and hired him. And they never used that test again. Joe was elated. This was the break he'd been working for. But it was a very heavy door -- with rusty hinges -- and Joe wasn't in yet.

As soon as he started in his new position, he pushed for skate parks.

Year after year he got the same response: "No, no, no." The powers that be insisted, "This is never going to happen."

When the city moved all Junior Recreation Leaders to Recreation Leaders, Joe moved up as well. As a Recreation Leader, he supervised every adult and kid league in the city. Although he didn't care much for his job, he stuck it out because of his goal. He kept pushing.

His directors had many concerns. They worried about the stigma associated with skate park kids. But most of all, they worried about kids hitting their heads on concrete at high speeds. The liability terrified them. They were not about to set the city up to be sued.

Wheelz

Then a congressman out of California, Senator Bill Morrow, passed a bill (SB 994) to permanently release liability of public city-owned skate parks by listing skateboarding as a hazardous recreational activity. Senator Morrow had heard what Joe was trying to do, so he called him for advice. After the law was passed, Nevada passed a similar bill.

When the law passed, every city councilman in Las Vegas wanted a skate park in his or her ward. Economically, the tax dollars were there. Some of the councilmen called Joe directly to ask how to get it done. It was totally inappropriate, but they did it anyway.

But the liability cap did not prevent lawsuits; it merely limited the damages. So Joe's directors continued to oppose him. They let him make proposals but had no intention of letting him actually build a park. The door was still effectively shut.

When he realized he'd never get approval, he formed a skate park coalition. He involved the Metropolitan Police Department, school districts, city council members, all skate and BMX shops, and anyone he could find in the community. He built an empire of influential people.

Our ward's city councilman, Larry Brown, was my son Brian's baseball coach. He was a great coach and a strong role model. Some of the opposing coaches were Neanderthals. They yelled

Wheelz

and swore at the umpires and even ostercized their own players. But not Larry. When a kid on the opposing team did something good, he praised him. When they made errors, he gave them suggestions. Because he was a class act, we did our share to help him get elected, and he turned out to be one of Joe's most supportive political officials. He did everything he could do to get skate parks in our area, but Joe was still opposed by his bosses.

Joe stopped putting proposals together that he knew would be turned down. Instead he planned festivals under the skate park coalition. The momentum of those events, involving so many influential people, began to open the door Joe had been powerless to move on his own.

His directors never did give him permission. They merely agreed to not stop him. They figured they could hide behind his coalition. That way, if they went down, the whole city would go down with them.

So with that backhanded approval, Joe started designing parks. He drew pictures and designs and gave them to the city architects. They drew up real plans from his sketches.

They asked, "Do we need to tweak this or do we need to tweak that?"

Joe showed them.

Wheelz

They wondered, "You didn't go to school for this?" Joe just smiled and said "No."

Once the plans were drawn, no one knew how to read them correctly. There were no local contractors who had built skate parks.

"We build pools," they said. "We do sidewalks."

Joe knew what they should look like, so he had to be involved in every step of the building process. He cut out plywood arches to show what he wanted because he couldn't explain it. He held the arches up and said, "Now, we need to add some concrete here and make it this shape."

Joe was on hand with a hammer and a trowel almost every day. His first parks didn't turn out the way he wanted, but they improved as he went along.

Over the years, Joe became a pro, designing million-dollar parks. People from all over the nation contacted him to design their parks or put ramps together. His work and advice became synonymous with professional skate park design, but in the beginning, it was touch and go. It was garage mechanics.

The parks, however, were only the first step. Joe wanted skateboarding and BMX-riding to be a sport like Little League or Pop Warner football, so he invented amateur jam sessions, the Vegas Am Jam. Each rider would take his turn, do a few tricks, then give someone else a turn. They'd have three, four, five rounds with each rider showing what he could do and watching what his peers were working on--like a band doing a jam session.

Joe decided to put BMXers and skateboarders, two groups who are notorious for hating each other, together. The city had wanted to split them up, but Joe followed his instincts. The bikers and skaters took their turns to show their own tricks and applauded their competitors. Instead of hating each other, they cheered each other on. The move encouraged camaraderie even in the midst of competition. It would also more easily accommodate a kid in a category of his own.

It facilitated the community Joe knew was essential to the survival of his sport. Just because he'd succeeded in building the parks didn't mean they couldn't be shut down. If he wanted to keep things alive and growing, he had to prove everyone's assumptions wrong.

So Joe showed up at each park regularly. At first glance, some of the kids mistook him for a policeman, with his muscular build and confident posture. But then they saw the straight blond hair that reached the middle of his back. He wasn't the law; he was a friend.

Wheelz

"You can keep this sport alive," he told the kids. "If there's something going bad at the skate park you need to tell me. These parks will be shut down as fast as they opened up. Trust me. I lived through it."

When Joe and his assistant Dana started Am Jam, they made and handed out flyers everywhere. They had t-shirts and stickers made. They got skateboards, wheels, bike tires, and other paraphernalia donated to hand out along with the trophies. When a kid won, he walked away with his arms full, and every category - beginner, intermediate, and advanced -had three winners.

Joe purchased a trailer that opened up like a concession stand and used it as a signup booth. He installed a P.A. system to make announcements and provide music for the meets. Next, bleachers were installed for parents and spectators. There was an ambulance on site for every competition. Eventually, Joe hired Ally to take Dana's place. She was also an amazing assistant.

Am Jam was the only extreme sports series in America at the time. Joe, Dana, and Ally made every event huge. The series lasted all year, with kids living solely for the next Am Jam session, which happened every two months and ended each year with finals.

After the Am Jam series became a success, Joe's bosses were forced to promote him. He had created a legitimate program that

Wheelz

required a supervisor to run it. Technically, Joe wasn't supposed to have the job that he had, but no one else knew how to run his series.

The city's solution was to create a supervisory position and fill it with a qualified candidate. City law requires that such positions are made available to the general public. In order to sort through these applicants, they needed to develop a test. As they wrote the test, Human Resources naturally turned to Joe for questions. He was their logical resource. He was their only resource.

Joe had concerns about taking a test he had essentially written, but since there wasn't a program like his, the city had no other options. And so he got the position, which is lucky for Las Vegas. No one else could have done what Joe did.

Joe must have known, in a vague way, his efforts would affect the kids at the skate parks. But he could not have known how much. He did not know there was someone whose life's ambitions would rely on his efforts.

Joe had no clue he was providing a platform for a kid on a wheelchair who was lacking just one thing--speed.

The Beginning

When Aaron was eight, the director of our adoption agency called me. "We have a child with spina bifida and hydrocephalus," he blurted out.

"Hydrocephalus?" I asked, not because I didn't know the term but because I needed a moment to process it. I knew hydrocephalus. When Aaron was a baby, he shared a recovery room with a hydrocephalic child in a coma.

Hydrocephalus means water on the brain. We all have a certain amount of cerebral-spinal fluid floating around our nervous system. That fluid is designed to move freely around the ventricles, or cavities, of the brain. But if there is an obstruction -- something that impedes the natural flow -- the fluid doesn't drain properly. It essentially builds up in the head and the head grows.

Before the medical field created shunts that could drain that fluid into the body, the outcome was always the same: the heads of hydrocephalic children grew until they couldn't grow anymore, and then they died. The shunts were a godsend. They saved many lives. But when they failed, the pressure on the child's brain could put him out of his mind--literally.
Aaron's roommate's shunt had failed. The doctors had to wait for the infection to subside before they dared put in a new one. As

they waited, the child's head swelled and he lapsed into unconsciousness.

His mother told us this was not their first time. Her sweet little boy was as normal as can be. He was a bright child. But when his shunts failed, he always followed the same inexorable course. First the headaches began. As the pressure/infection roller coaster took its toll, he increasingly lost his mind until he was totally gone.

Many children with spina bifida have hydrocephalus. When we heard her story, I remember thinking, *Thank God Aaron doesn't have that.* Now the adoption agency was calling us with the H-word.

"He has hydrocephalus," he said. "We've tried every avenue we know to find him a home. We've tried the state. We've tried all our clients. We know you have experience with spina bifida. If you don't adopt him, nobody will."

When he put it that way, what choice did we have?

We took the whole family to the hospital to meet the baby, which, in retrospect, might not have been the best idea. They strolled and rolled and tiptoed up to the nursery window, peering through the glass at an infant in a warming unit.

Wheelz

Half of his head had been shaved to reveal a marble-sized bump with a tube running down his head just under his skin. His eyes were black and blue from his recent operation.

Lisa took one look and said, "He looks like a devil child."

"Lisa," Kaylene scolded.

"Actually," I said, "he does look like a devil child." No point in sugarcoating things; the kid had spina bifida *and* hydrocephalus. We went home to talk about it.

"If you don't adopt him, nobody will" kept running through my mind. I might have dismissed that thought as absurd, but something I had heard the day before wouldn't let me. A leader in our church had spoken about "defining moments" that require us to make "on-the-record" choices. Our responses to our allotted tests, he said, are "what matter" [iv]

Those words out of a two-day, ten-hour conference had stuck with me more than anything else. Now they were pinning us in a corner. We had no doubt this was a defining moment. It was also clear how we responded mattered immensely to this child and our God. It was an "on-the-record" decision, which meant if we wanted to be true to our beliefs we didn't have a choice at all.

With Mikey we were already overwhelmed. I thought, *What a rip. We didn't ask for this.* Kaylene wasn't praying for another child. So what was this? Didn't God know our plate was already full? I was resentful. This time I was sure my life was over. If He thought so little of my life why should I be overly concerned for it? We were old enough now to know that our road, no matter how hard, would not be unbearably long; there was a light at the end of the tunnel and that light was death. I actually counted what I figured might be my remaining years and thought, *Oh, well.*

So long before we had ever heard of a MegaRamp, we found ourselves on top of one for a second time. And notwithstanding our first attempt, with Aaron, turned out well, this ramp was higher. All we could see was down and we were terrified! When we realized our only choice was to jump, I called the director.

"We'll adopt him if the state will pay his medical bills," I said.

"No problem," he answered immediately.

"What you did was wrong," I said. "You should never put anyone in a corner like that."

"I know."

"Don't ever do that to us again. Don't ever do that to anyone again."

Wheelz

He was humble. "I know. I'm sorry. But in my defense, it worked."

I couldn't argue with that. We adopted the child and named him Joseph.

The truth is flying down a huge ramp is exhilarating. Flying over the gap is amazing. And if by chance, by some miracle, you stick the landing, there are few greater moments in life. In those moments you are never more alive. You have so many wonderful thoughts. But there is also one shuttering thought: *What if we had backed down?*

Our first miracle with Joey came when we took him to meet Dr. Smith and friends at Primary Children's Hospital. When we expressed our fears to Dr. Smith, what we had seen with that mother and her son, he informed us we had nothing to worry about.

He told us, "Shunts have come a long way since then." He smiled broadly at our skeptical faces. "You'll see."

Within a year, we put Dr. Smith's confidence to the test. Joey's first shunt failed. We took him back to Primary Children's.

"No problem," the doctor replacing the shunt said.

Wheelz

"What about infection?" Kayene asked.

"We don't care if there's an infection. We'll put the new shunt in on the other side of his head and bypass any infection." Then the doctor expressed surprise that Joey's previous shunt was so big. Kaylene could tell he was holding back what he was thinking.

When Kaylene pressed the issue he said, "You need to remember we're a children's hospital. We probably do more shunts in a month than most hospitals do in a couple years. That shunt is an old model. Like so many technological advances in our day, they are now smaller, completely unnoticeable, and more efficient."

After the operation Kaylene expressed surprise when they hadn't shaved his head. She was told shaving the head was also a thing of the past. Everything was good. Hydrocephalus quickly became something that we didn't have to worry about.

Joey had some challenges from his spina bifida, but they were minor. With his hair grown in and his eyes no longer bruised, he was a beautiful child.

We assumed he wouldn't walk. But his legs didn't flail out to his sides like a frog's. And when he was old enough to crawl, he crawled. When it came time for him to learn to walk, he walked. He did have low muscle tone in one foot and ankle. That required

Wheelz

a brace, that was it. He could walk fine. He had some challenges, he did have spina bifida, but compared to Aaron's, Joey's medical complications were minor. The adoption agency had sold us on how much he needed us. It turned out we desperately needed him.

Our family consisted of me, two teenage kids with their own challenges, a passionate kid with anger issues, two kids with attachment problems (one of them being Mikey), and one frazzled wife. But this last child had a gift. He was kind.

As a toddler, he seemed to know where he was needed. He'd crawl through the house until he found Kaylene in our bedroom. She was chronically overwhelmed and exhausted. A number of times he found her collapsed on the floor, crying. On those occasions, Joey would climb into her lap, wrap his little arms around her, and hold her. He didn't let go until she was okay.

Once Kaylene burnt the bottom of one of her good sauce pans. She scrubbed the black bottom, but it didn't come clean. That took her over the top of an already hard day. She went to our room, shut the door, and cried. I had learned to let her be for a while.
But this time I picked up little Joe, cracked open the door, put him in on his knees, and closed the door behind him.
He found her in a corner of her room and melted her into peace. It was like he knew his job was to save her. Indeed we were sure he knew because he would lean away from her to catch her eyes;

Wheelz

he would even cup her cheeks with his little hands to get her to look into his face. He would then smile, not a childish smile, but a gentle smile and then pull himself in to hold her.

It was that look with the hug that told us he knew what he was doing. I have never heard of or seen anything like this. As he grew, when we would ask him to do something, like get ready for bed, he'd say, "Okay."

Kaylene and I would look at each other like, "What was that?"
He didn't challenge us. All of our other children, especially Aaron, were so strong willed and frankly at times difficult to live with. This one was just a sweet, obedient child. He still is. So far he has not lost his gift.

I have apologized to God for resenting him. I have imagined angels looking on while we thought we were making some huge sacrifice, doing him a big favor. They must have thought, *That's nice.* We have never been able to get Him in our debt. I have often wondered, *What if we had not gotten Joey?* and shuddered at the thought.

During those years, even with Joey, we still wondered what we'd gotten ourselves into. While Kaylene was trudging through an emotional wasteland, giving more than she had to give, I was enjoying my dream job. I was at that time teaching at the Institute of Religion adjacent to The University of Nevada at Las Vegas

Wheelz

(UNLV). All day long I taught, counseled, and joked around with bright college students. Since I never came home with an empty cup, I saw it as my job to fill hers.

Eighteen-year-old Lisa spent most of her time with the drama department at school. Brian, aged fourteen, loved riding BMX at the skate parks. I was glad he had something to do that didn't require much from his parents. Aaron usually rolled around the neighborhood with his friends. My cup-filling mainly entailed getting Mikey and Christina out of the house, so I frequented our neighborhood parks.

One Saturday, after a typically exhausting week, I set out to give my wife a break. Brian was headed to Metro Park, so I told Kaylene I'd take Mikey and Christina to watch him. Aaron said he'd come along. We piled in the car and drove to the park, Christina wondered aloud what she'd do when she arrived, Mikey and Aaron staring out the window, and me hoping Joey would find my wife sooner rather than later.

The fence around the Metro Skate Park has vertical bars like a prison cell. I liked them because they kept Mikey away from the riders. I sat on a concrete picnic bench under a metal canopy and watched Brian. Aaron rode on the sidewalk outside of the fence. He'd pump his wheels until he was flying down the sidewalk, then spin around on one wheel and fly back up on two.

Wheelz

It was a beautiful day. Most days are in the land of eternal sunshine. There is a cold month or two in the winter, and a couple of months in the summer are unbearably hot, but the weather is generally ideal for riders. Even in those hot summer months, the desert evenings are cool enough to ride on the heat-drenched concrete. This day was warm, with a light breeze and enough clouds to dampen the glare of the sun.

As my attention rotated from Brian to Aaron to Mikey, I thought about my patchwork family and the unique challenges of putting so many adopted kids -- all with different needs -- together under one roof. It was tough, but I tried to appreciate what went right. For example, I felt incredibly blessed that Brian and Lisa had always treated Aaron like a regular brother. He made it difficult to view him otherwise.

I remembered a time one Christmas, while the family was unwrapping presents, when Aaron grabbed a discarded bow and stuck it to his forehead.

Brian smirked at him.

"I'm a present," Aaron said.

"What a rip," Brian responded, pulling the bow off Aaron and gesturing in his direction. "It's broken."

Lisa smiled and Aaron laughed.

Years later we were sitting around the table talking about all the media attention Aaron was getting.

Lisa quipped, "That's great, but you still can't walk." Aaron loved that.

He expected Brian to pound on him like any big brother would, and Brian always obliged. He would push Aaron over in his chair to the floor then hit him repeatedly. Aaron would laugh, but Brian wouldn't stop until Aaron cried out for him to stop. I was constantly telling Brian to stop crossing the line. And yet in a strange way treating Aaron like he did was a show of respect. That wasn't lost on Aaron.

One day Kaylene told Brian to stop beating on him and teasing him so mercilessly. A few days later Brian said, "Mom, we need to talk. If I don't do this he'll be a wuss. He'll never survive middle school." We didn't realize he was being so calculated.

Kaylene said, "I'll try to back off."

I wasn't surprised, then, when Aaron wanted to watch Brian working jumps at the park. The sound of Brian calling to his brother pulled me from my wandering thoughts.

"Hey, Aaron! Come over here and try this."

I looked up. I was not alarmed, but curious about Aaron's reaction. He rolled his chair to the bottom of the ramp. Brian signaled to a couple of his friends. They pushed Aaron up to the platform at the top. He rolled to the edge, hesitated for a few seconds, and then went over.

His chair slid through the silence, down the ramp, as Brian and his friends watched eagerly. At the bottom, his front wheels caught a ridge, and he went flying to the ground on his face and wrists. I heard the sound of metal scraping across concrete, felt my breath catch in my throat for an instant, and waited. Brian's crew was silent; everyone falls at skate parks, especially the first time, no matter what the vehicle.

"Cool," said Brian. "Go again?"

Aaron nodded. He climbed back into his chair and they pushed him up for another try. His front wheels were tripping him up, so he went down the second time on only his back wheels. There was another sprawl, his forearms taking the brunt this time.

"Again," Aaron said.

They pushed him up again. I moved a little closer for a better view, resting my arms on that fence. Brian and his friends didn't

Wheelz

say much. They certainly didn't wince or groan when Aaron hit the ground; they all knew the price of mastering a trick. Aaron's eyes were bright with excitement and filled with determination. He knew, we knew, he would master that ramp.

Skate parks are addicting. There is no better way to put it.

Years later I once said to Brian, at the very same park, "Let me try your bike." He smirked and said, "Go ahead."

I rode down the ramp Aaron had started on. I followed my momentum and started to go up another ramp. The bike slid right out from under me. That's when I got the revelation that skate parks are smooth as glass. If you can stay up on a bike or a board or a wheelchair, it is like floating on smooth marble. It is easy to see how a kid can be instantly hooked on shredding the ramps.

I didn't count the number of times he missed or how many bruises he racked up before he landed it. I only remember that he wouldn't stop until he did. And all it took was that first time -- just one single success -- to start a sport he would one day define.

Speed

"If you can read this, lift me up! Please!" – Aaron Fotheringham, on the bottom of his chair.

For a kid who could already do so many flat-ground tricks, skate parks were heaven. The exhilaration of speed, the thrill of learning new tricks, the support of friends who saw him as one of them, the skate park on cool Vegas nights lit up like a ball field, all gave Aaron a new home--a new life perfectly suited to his attitude about himself and his chair.

Like every biker or skateboarder, Aaron learned one trick at a time. He practiced for hours every day. He progressed in leaps and bounds. I was amazed every time I went to watch him. But all that practice took its toll on a chair that wasn't built for what Aaron was doing.

Rebecca Volle, a friend who rotated through our multitude of carpools, noticed his beat up chair. By that time, it was held together with duct tape. She stowed it in the back of her car, dropped Aaron off at school, and went home to talk to her husband. The next evening, Dan Volle knocked on my door. After a few initial pleasantries, he got right to the point.

"We've got a group of people together who want to get Aaron a new chair." he said.

"His chair is fine," I said, thinking about the 6000-dollar price tag attached to sport wheelchairs. "There's air in the tires and the seat's level. What more could a kid want?"

"It's not fine." Dan said, smiling. "We insist."

"Do you understand the cost of what you're suggesting?"

He nodded with a peculiar gleam in his eye. I knew there was nothing more to argue about. So Aaron got his first Colours wheelchair.

He hated it at first, but then he always hated his new chairs until he broke them in. Like a new pair of running shoes or a new set of guitar strings, new wheelchairs had to be softened a bit. He had to get the feel for them. The Colours wheelchair was amazing, and it didn't take Aaron long to adjust. His annoyance morphed into love as he adjusted to the added suspension that gave him more stability and flexibility. His world had grown a little wider.

So with a new vehicle, he set to work on learning better tricks. In the beginning, I was his videographer. He practiced for days until he was ready, and then I'd take him to each park to record his progress.

Wheelz

On a whim, I sent one of his DVDs to Colours Wheelchairs. 'Thought you might want to see what my boy is doing with your chair," I wrote.

The owner, John Box, called Kaylene. "If your boy needs anything call me."

He had no clue what that gesture of kindness would cost his company. Aaron would need more than any client they had or would ever have. But at that time we had no clue what his offer meant. We figured if we had a bent axle, he would help us out.

A few months later Kaylene called back. "My son has tweaked his chair. Is it possible to get it straightened?"

"No," John replied with a dramatic pause, "what you need to do is come to California and we'll make him a new one."

So we drove to California to meet the Box brothers. It was a pivotal moment for Aaron's career and one of his happiest days on record. When we arrived, both John and Mike came out to meet us -- well, me and Kaylene, really. If they expected eleven-year-old Aaron to sit calmly in his chair and shake their hands then they didn't know him at all. On top of that, they shouldn't have built the parking lot they had built -- long and flat, with concrete parking barriers, curbs, and sidewalks with ramps. Aaron

Wheelz

was long gone -- spinning, jumping, and speeding up and down the black pavement.

The Colours company slogan was "Enjoy the Ride." The message insinuated by the pictures in their brochures was basically, "You can be a model, a motocross rider, a body builder, a guy parachuting, even though you're in a chair." They wanted people to understand that life goes on in spite of a disability, life is great -- enjoy the ride.

But Aaron came with a philosophy of his own, one that helped expand their vision and their sales. And like the pictures in Colours brochures, he didn't say anything. His message was loud and clear, plastered across his face as he cruised their parking lot: the most enjoyable ride was their chair.

So while Aaron practiced I got to know the Box brothers. John Box had been in a wheelchair since he was a teenager, when a hit-and-run accident left him a paraplegic. His brother, Mike, was an engineer/welder who had worked on military projects like the stealth bomber and large-caliber weapons. Both men had big hearts and big dreams.

John's dream started when he approached a large wheelchair manufacturer and requested a custom chair.

"We don't do custom chairs," the company spokesperson replied.

Wheelz

"Well, perhaps you could consider it," John pled.

"Nope. Company policy."

Their reaction angered John, but it also inspired him. He decided he and his brother should make their own chairs. With Mike's mechanical abilities and John's business acumen, he figured they'd make a good team. They started Colours Wheelchairs, and before long they were competing with the company who had turned him down.

Life had been hard on Mike Box. When we met him, he was on his fourth marriage. Two of his wives had died and the third had divorced him. He had turned to alcohol, which only made things worse. But when we met Mike, he was deeply in love with his new bride and had been sober for years.

John and Mike had much greater ambitions for their company than merely selling wheelchairs. The bigger they got, the more opportunities they had to help. They provided hundreds of inexpensive wheelchairs to children in third-world countries. When they believed there was a need, they gave a number of their custom chairs away as well.

But while I had never met such a generous team, they had never met anyone like Aaron. They seemed as pleased to meet him as we were to meet them.

"He's a pro," they said to me. "We've never seen anyone with these kinds of skills on a chair." And when he wasn't around, they confided in me, "He seems like a good kid -- not too full of himself -- even though he could be, considering what he can do."

Aaron was not overly proud. But he was an attention junky. When he was young and we'd had a good day together he would get angry when the day was done. That in turn made me angry— he knew the right buttons to push—my scolding him would in turn give him more attention.

"He's really just grateful to be here." I said. And he was.

Once we convinced Aaron to come into the building, Mike and Aaron got to work. In the middle of the showroom floor, amid all the shiny, new wheelchairs and company logos gracing the walls, Mike Box sat down cross-legged with a notepad in his lap. He measured Aaron's legs and examined his chair.

"What do you want in a chair?" he asked.

Aaron brought out a list and laughed self-consciously. I sighed in the background. The list was long. I feared he was asking for too much.

"Could you put a grinding bar under the suspension?" he asked.

"Maybe you should be gentler on your chair," I interrupted, not wanting Mike to think we would abuse their generosity.

Mike looked up at me. He had the rugged face of a construction worker with a slight smile. "Lighten up, Dad. If he breaks it, we'll make him another one."

I didn't say anything. Aaron went back to the details of the grinding bar as Mike took notes. That was the beginning of a wonderful relationship. For the next several years, Aaron beat his Colours chairs to death. He became their test dummy. In turn, Mike kept improving the design.

It took a great deal of time and patience, but the continual improvements -- especially the added suspension -- did far more than simply improve Aaron's comfort. Outfitted with such a well-designed piece of equipment, Aaron learned to fly. When he'd drop into a bowl, he'd fall a few feet before he contacted the curve of it. I don't know if he held his breath or not during that half-second of freefall. I always did. And, of course, he had to keep his front wheels out of the way until he reached the bottom curve of the bowl. One slip and he'd be back on the ground, his chair spinning angrily off to the side while some new body part grew intimately acquainted with the concrete.

As his chairs got tougher, he got tougher. He took his sport to new heights -- literally. I remember the first time he attempted a ten-foot drop. He balanced on the edge for a long time. I wasn't sure he would actually go through with it.

He was afraid, but it wasn't fear stopping him. He hesitated on the edge because he needed time to ride the drop in his mind. He didn't want to be stupid. He needed to focus. When he finally nudged his chair over that edge, he must have dropped four feet before his back wheels touched the curve, and he was traveling faster than he had ever traveled before. He landed it perfectly. It took only a few more tries before the trick was mastered and added to his repertoire. He was relentless in pursuit of this mastery in spite of the toll it took on his body.

One skate park had a drop that led to a spine (a quarter pipe that has a three-inch ledge at the top with another quarter pipe on the other side). Aaron wanted me to tape him going up and over the spine. He tried dozens of times. He got high enough at the top of the ramp, but then he had to lunge his chair forward to cross to the other side. He smashed his shins and forearms on that ledge repeatedly.

The pain, however, seemed incidental to his frustration and anger at getting so close and not succeeding. He didn't master it that day, but we both knew it would be only a matter of time. A couple weeks later I saw him clear a spine with a foot to spare. He made it look so natural and so easy, as if his chair just floated up and forward on its own. Years later he would do a backflip over a spine.

Of course, mastering that trick -- and all of the others -- meant that Aaron spent hours and hours at the parks. I think he would have attracted some attention if he'd been on a skateboard or a bike. But in a wheelchair, he drew everybody's notice. Even before Joe Wichert began Am Jam, he knew Aaron. They met while hanging out at some of the festivals that Aaron attended.

Joe liked what he saw in this kid. With skate parks dotting Las Vegas and a full blown Am Jam league, Joe had met his goals. Now he had a new one; getting that kid in a wheelchair to compete.

Am Jam

Aaron knew who Joe was too, but in the beginning he wanted nothing to do with him. Joe often found him wheeling down Alexander Road to Pro or Bunker Parks. Whenever he saw Aaron, he pulled over to the side of the road.

"Hey, do you want a ride to the park?" he'd ask. Aaron pretended not to hear him.

Joe tried to talk to him at the skate parks, too. His assistant, Dana, laughed at him. "He's not going to talk to you," she said.

"He doesn't have to," Joe answered. "I'll just talk to him."

Anytime Aaron was around, Joe talked. Aaron looked down, looked around, looked anywhere except at Joe, but Joe knew he was listening. Every chance he had, he said, "Hey, Aaron, how's it going?" He didn't expect a reply.

Joe gave Aaron t-shirts and stickers, anything he could find as a plausible excuse to talk to the kid. Joe realized that Aaron knew all of the other kids at the parks. He had no problem talking to them, but an adult butting in on their turf was just weird.

Joe knew Aaron wanted to be involved in the competitions, but he sensed Aaron's hesitation. Aaron wasn't on a skateboard or on

Wheelz

a bike. Joe had to get past that. He figured he needed to help Aaron see where he could fit in.

During one conversation, when he actually succeeded in eliciting a response, Joe asked, "Do you want to enter the competition?"

Aaron shook his head.

"Why not?" Joe asked.

Aaron didn't answer.

Joe continued, "Just because you're in a chair? It's got wheels, right?"

"Yeah."

"So you pick your category. Skateboards got wheels like yours; BMX's got wheels like yours. Whatever you feel you want to go into."

Aaron wheeled away without answering.
But the next time Aaron saw him, Joe asked, "Are you ready to do this? I'll sign you up."

Aaron shook his head, waved his hand at him, and wheeled off. The answer was always "no."

Wheelz

Joe thought Aaron was intimidated by the thought of the crowd, so he tried to reassure him. "You're not going out there by yourself, Aaron. You're going out there with all these kids. Not everyone's focusing on you. The judges are watching all the kids. Don't think you're on stage giving a speech. It's not that embarrassing."

But that wasn't it. "I'm not afraid of performing in front of the people," Aaron explained to his mom. She wasn't surprised. This kid, the one who walked on his hands at parks, loved crowds. "I'm afraid of winning."

"What do you mean? Why wouldn't you want to win?"

"All those kids are my friends. They'd hate losing to a kid in a chair. These are the guys who help push me out of the bowls. If I beat them, then what will they think?"

Kaylene nodded thoughtfully.

"What if the judges give me an unfair advantage? Just because I'm in a chair? That wouldn't be right."

But Aaron loved to ride. He got better every day, and the competitive side of him -- as well as the attention seeking side of him -- was urging him on. Little by little, he warmed up to Joe.

Wheelz

Sometimes he stopped by the trailer to say hello. Of course, as soon as Joe and Dana responded, greeted him, asked if he wanted any help, he wheeled away. But it was a start.

He fascinated Joe. Though Joe was not overly competitive himself, he sensed that Aaron was. Despite Dana's advice to leave the kid alone, Joe couldn't. He liked having Aaron shredding at his parks. He liked the determination in his eyes. He had never seen so much drive in a kid so young. So he compromised. He talked to Aaron about other things, asked his opinion, and engaged him in conversation whenever he could. And the more they talked, the more Joe realized that Aaron wanted to be part of Am Jam.

His hesitation stemmed from his questions about the competition. Joe had to convince him that he would be judged only on the variety of his tricks and degree of difficulty.

"I guess," Aaron told his mom. "If that's really how I'll be judged -- you know, difficulty versus difficulty -- I guess I can compete."

He went to see Joe. "Okay. I'm ready."

Joe composed his face into what he hoped was a nonchalant expression. "What class?"

"BMX."

Joe nodded. "Smart choice. You've got the big wheels. It's similar to your frame—more similar to BMX, so we'll put you in BMX."

Aaron started competing. And Joe was true to his word; the judging was based on skill and variety -- nothing more -- which meant Aaron didn't win at first, though he made great progress. His thirst for competency was insatiable and he clearly stopped at nothing to master his tricks.

This drive impressed Joe, but it also concerned him. Aaron's body was taking a lot of hits when he missed a trick.

As he watched Aaron compete one afternoon, Joe realized he needed to get this guy a helmet—a real helmet, not a skateboard helmet—because he was hitting the deck hard.

He told Aaron, "Man, you really need a full face helmet. You need to protect yourself."

BMXers usually wore what they called "brain buckets." It was open-faced and more of a skater helmet. But Joe had seen some of the more aggressive kids wear full face helmets and encouraged Aaron to upgrade.

When Aaron found a used, ratty, fullface helmet, I thought he was fine. After all, I could see he was more protected than any other kid in the park. Joe knew better.

Wheelz

"You need to get a better helmet," he told Aaron. "You're going to hurt yourself. We've got to get you something that's going to protect your head."

Aaron nodded vaguely. He was fully aware of the price tag attached to helmets, and as one of six children, he knew better than to ask for one.

But Joe wouldn't let up about it. He hounded Aaron regularly about getting a new helmet and gloves for his hands. "You need to use gloves. You can't do this every day. You're developing calluses and eventually you're going to wear through them and start bleeding and hurting."

Once again, Aaron just shrugged.

I knew who Joe was from seeing him at the skate parks. He fit in perfectly there. He was a California surfer, a BMXer, and a skateboarder like all the other kids at the park -- just a bit older. I knew he was in charge of things and I knew he was a nice guy. I thanked him often for what he was doing for the kids--my son included. But I did not know him well. Then one evening, he knocked at our door.

I opened it to see his silhouette framed in the doorway, the porch light cascading over his shoulders and down his arms to rest on

Wheelz

his brand new helmet and gloves in his hands. "I'd like to sponsor your son," he said. "I really believe in him and want to promote what he's doing."

Aaron rolled up behind me, so I stepped aside to let Joe give him the gear.

"Thanks."

"No problem." Joe turned to me. "When he wears these out I'll get him more."

Aaron and I stayed in the open doorway while Joe walked back to his truck and drove away. His kindness moved me, but I didn't truly understand it. I thought Aaron's interest in skate parks was like Brian's: fun for the moment but nothing more. I didn't understand why Joe had gone to the effort and expense of buying him a helmet and gloves or why he worried about Aaron more than any of the other kids goofing around at the parks all day.

But Joe saw much more than I did, and because of that he was willing to back Aaron more than I was. I never even considered that he might need better equipment, let alone a helmet sponsor. It would be years before I saw what Joe saw in my son. But Aaron didn't have time to wait for me. He went through helmets faster than my other children went through shoes, and he knew we couldn't afford 300 to 400 dollars every other month, so he never asked.

Joe stepped in to help him instead, though it soon became evident that he couldn't afford him either. He was in over his head. He checked the inner lining in Aaron's helmets every time they met. If the foam was compressed, and it was often compressed, he needed a new one. So Joe paid a visit to Sam Abraham at Sam's Cycle Supply. "I've got this kid Aaron," he explained. "Can you help me out?"

Sam offered to talk to some of his suppliers. He gave Aaron a couple helmets off his shelves to keep him going, but the suppliers were not as eager to help as Sam and Joe were. Many people see kids in wheelchairs as fragile. The companies Sam talked to were not keen on the idea of Aaron getting injured while wearing their equipment. It would be like their protective equipment wasn't protective enough. They liked what he was doing, but backing him was too risky. Joe and Sam persisted. Finally, Six Six One agreed to sponsor him.

So Aaron got helmets and Joe slept a little easier at night. When the first set of gloves wore out, Aaron said nothing to Joe. He knew no one could afford to keep him in gloves when he went through a pair a week, so he figured his calluses would just have to develop calluses. But he did love the helmets. Now and then he came home with a new helmet and put his stickers on it. I

Wheelz

thought, *That's nice*. I had no idea how hard the community was working to support my son.

I was also unaware that the hits on Joe's city website were all about Aaron. From all over, with or without disabilities, they'd say, "If he can aspire to his dreams, I can aspire to mine." Joe and Ally, his new assistant, read them and said, "This is crazy."

WHEELZ

"Success is not final, failure is not fatal: it is the courage to continue that counts." Winston Churchill

Aaron wanted me to video tape him at Bunker Park. I was so clueless, I didn't understand why there was a number pinned to his back and such a big crowd. No one told me he was competing.

He flew over a rung of steps leading into the base of the park. He hit a few jumps, dropped in and did some spins. He then got a good run at the top of the concrete and ground down a concrete wall. The wall was about three feet high and twelve feet long and it sloped downward. At the end it dropped about two feet into the bowl. I wondered how he learned that trick without falling on his face several times. He told me his friends spotted him on both sides until he could regularly make it.

He slid down that wall with his hands out like an airplane for balance. In a short time he would ride that grind with his hands clasped behind his helmet. It was his version of "Look, no hands!" He honed every trick like a gymnast.

A few competitions later he did a trick that astounded me. He tilted his chair backwards as if to lay the back of his seat on the concrete, but he kept it just off the ground. At the same time, he slid to the front of his seat and sat on the thin edge, all while balancing on his two back wheels. His chin was even with his two front wheels.

Once he was perched on the top of his seat, he proceeded to roll down a ramp in that position. That ramp ended in a two-foot drop into the bowl. When he landed in the bowl, the force threw him backwards to the concrete, but no one cared; it was an amazing stunt. He was twelve at the time. It was at that moment I started to see what Joe saw.

He was continually doing bigger and more jaw-dropping things. For instance, the Pro Park slopes down at a pretty good angle from the west to the east. The north platform is long and slick. My wife saw and loved the trick when he posted it on YouTube. He got a long run at the top of the park then yanked his chair sideways for a power slide. He slid at least eighty-feet and it was beautiful. I don't believe a kid on a bike or a board could go more than a couple feet without tipping over. With his broad wheel base it was easy, or at least he made it look easy. It is one of those tricks that caused his friends to sincerely say, "I wish I was in a wheelchair."

VIDEO 2: A video of some of his early competitions
http://goo.gl/AgiO7E

"When I first started going to school," Aaron explained in a documentary, "they would always ask if I wanted to be put into adaptive P.E. (physical education) with other kids on wheelchairs. I was always against that because I thought, *Well, I'm just like every other kid. I'm just on a wheelchair.* So I would always fight and make them put me in regular P.E. The coaches were always pumped because I'd always be there. I just wanted to do what the other kids were doing. I think that was an important part, having nobody treat me any different."

When the coaches had the kids run laps, they told Aaron he didn't have to, but he wouldn't hear of it. He ran the laps with his crutches. "He just wants to be seen as an athlete," Kaylene explained to reporters, "not pigeonholed as a disabled athlete."

As a little boy, when our neighbors climbed a small mountain in our area, he climbed it with them. They wouldn't have thought of leaving him behind any more than he would have considered staying. As a Boy Scout, he went on every hike his troop went on with his crutches. When they rode mountain bikes, he went to a local skate park. On occasions when he needed help, he accepted help. But most of the time he kept up just fine.

He and his brother shared a bunk bed and Aaron took the top bunk. Every night, he pulled himself up the side rails using only his arms. In the morning he dove off headfirst, landing on his hands on the floor.

By the time that Aaron hit his teens, he wouldn't even think about special accommodations. We visited a disabled dealer's convention in Anaheim, California, where they had several displays of retrofitted vans for wheelchairs. I thought they were pretty neat, and I was heartened by the thought that Aaron would have so many options when he was old enough to drive. Aaron, to my surprise, wanted nothing to do with them. He was insulted when I brought them up. He wanted a truck like any respectable BMXer would drive.

When he could drive, he got that truck, outfitting it with hand controls so he could drive without using his feet. But there were no hydraulic wheelchair lifts, no special options to make things more accessible. This decision meant he had to hang onto the side of his truck with one arm while he threw his chair up and into the back with the other.

And because he had the mindset of a biker, he had to have his truck tricked-out. So he bought huge wheels and jacked up his suspension. Then he had to throw his chair a couple of feet higher to get it into the bed of the truck. It was a small price to pay for having a cool ride.

He would not let the fact that he couldn't walk get in the way of anything he wanted to do. At the same time, if there was an advantage of being on a chair he'd gobble it up. If there was a cute girl, he was the poor kid in a wheelchair. He could play at the skate park all day, but when it came time to clean his room, he was disabled. At an early age, he knew he could score as a beggar. He once bought a bank at Target and had three quarters in it before he reached the register. When we used handicapped parking spots, he'd say, "It's cool they make parking spots just for me." We would always thank him for being crippled and getting us preferred parking.

We offered him to family and friends who were going to Disneyland; being let in at the front of the line was fine with him. We once forgot to bring matches on a camping trip, so of course, Aaron was sent to get some from other camps. He enjoyed playing the little pauper: "Please, sir, could we borrow some matches?" On Saturdays, we visited garage sales. People seldom let Aaron pay. He thought it was all great, so long as they didn't tell him what he couldn't do. He refused to be forced to the sidelines because he was on a chair.

Wheelz

Aaron grew up to become a professional extreme sport athlete. I think his desire to be like his biker friends, the fact that he grew up in their world, had much to do with his success. The fact that he was on a wheelchair also drove him because he wasn't about to compete in their world as a tag-along. We'll never know all that was behind his drive, but he had the drive of any kid who aspired to be and eventually became a pro. In other words, he worked his butt off.

Thomas Edison said, "Opportunity is missed by most people because it is dressed in overalls and looks like work." My son has had so many wonderful opportunities. He has earned every one of them.

For example, the rainbow-shaped grinding bar at the Pro Park is seventeen feet long. He wanted to grind the entire length of that bar and just couldn't get there.

He started the trick with a 40-foot downhill run at the bar at full speed. He hit it with the front of his chair and ground on the rainbow up and forward for about ten feet. It always looked like he would make it, but inevitably, he ran out of speed. Those runs always ended in the same way -- with Aaron crashing on his face and his side, his heavy chair pushing him into the concrete. I don't know how many times he crashed it on his own. It must have been at least fifty. Once he thought he was close, he asked me to come and film him.

I watched through the camera lens as he tried it at least a dozen times without success. He was so determined, so frustrated, so angry that it was hard to watch him. The balance had to be perfect, but he also needed enough speed to grind the length of the rail. No matter how hard he pushed his chair, he wasn't getting the speed he needed. He did not hit it that day. I would have given up. The rainbow grind isn't part of the skate park, really, so he couldn't use it during competition. What was the point?

He worked on the grind until he landed it, but that wasn't enough. He needed to be able to land it all the time, every time. When he did, he got a friend to follow him on a skateboard with his camera. All those hours, all those crashes. The video was amazing, but eventually, that trick became just another one in his growing repertoire.

Whenever a news station interviewed him, he gave them access to his videos. The rainbow footage was on his DVDs. I would guess by now that millions have seen that video. He makes it look so easy. He makes it look fun. That, ultimately, is the point

They started calling him "Wheels" in junior high. Aaron liked the name, but he changed it to "Wheelz" with a "Z." He began signing his name with a wheelchair design.

Wheelz

He once told me, "My friends all have to leave their bikes at the gate when they come to school. I get to ride mine anywhere I want."

One day in junior high, Aaron took his camera and helmet. The school officials did not condone him jumping the stairs. They scolded and threatened him when he tried. But one of the custodians understood.

When no one was looking, he told Aaron, "Now, you stay away from those stairs while I'm going to the office to take care of some things."

Word got out that Aaron was going to jump the stairs after school. He was surprised to see a crowd of kids line both sides of the jump. The jump required a long running start inside the school. That meant two kids had to hold the doors open at the end of the run right before the stairs. One of those kids was Joe Wichert's son, Trevor. Aaron pushed as fast as he could through the doors and flew out over and beyond the stairs. When I measured the distance later, I realized he had traveled about twelve feet in the air with only about three feet of drop to safely clear the bottom step. I was amused, however, to find out that the principal called Joe, not me. He figured Joe was somehow behind Aaron's stunts. He was right.

Wheelz

Aaron lived at the skate parks. But he didn't need a park to play. Like any biker or skateboarder, every curb is a trick and every step is a jump. If he found a puddle on a sidewalk, he would hit it at full speed then turn his chair sideways and slide for several feet in a power slide. Every speed bump, every concrete parking bumper, any change in the road became something to bounce off of or jump over.

I saw him once riding down Buffalo Avenue, heading for the Pro Park on the sidewalk. It was a beautiful, cool evening -- the perfect night to ride. I was driving in his direction, and he was going fast enough that I could stay behind him, so he didn't know I was there. He swerved back and forth like a skier, flew over the curb into the intersection and back up the curb onto the sidewalk on the other side. It was obvious from his movements he was listening to his music. And it was obvious he was having fun. A BMXer's mother told me her son was saving up to get a chair like Aaron's.

One day at the end of 2005, Aaron needed me to come to Metro Park, where he had gone down that first ramp with his brother, to sign a waiver for a competition. He asked me for a couple bucks to buy a drink. I handed him the money and, in a voice loud enough for his friends to hear, said, "Don't come home unless you have a first-place trophy." He laughed. I left.

Wheelz

When I came home that night, there was a BMX Intermediate Class trophy on our entry hutch. It was his first win, and it was first place. And though he failed to mention it -- indeed, he never brought it up at all -- it was the series final.

Aaron was not the first to ride a wheelchair down a ramp any more than Tony Hawk was the first to ride a skateboard. Nevertheless, he was the first to turn it into a sport. He first named the sport Crazy Cripple Industries, a name that lasted until he saw there was a company named CCI. He then named it Hardcore Sitting. All he needed was to get the word out. That would take only one trick.

A Backflip

Aaron had talked to his mom about doing a backflip. She'd listened with growing apprehension, even though he never once suggested he'd practice on concrete. It was the elephant in the room between them for a while.

"No way," she said. "This isn't like the other tricks. You'll have to find some kind of gym or something. Somewhere with a foam pit or a net so you don't kill yourself."

Then she attended an Am Jam competition where Joe offered the prize of a partially paid week at Woodward West in California.

"What is Woodward?" Kaylene asked Joe after the competition.

"It's a camp for skaters and BMXers," he explained. "You know, ramps, obstacles, and stuff, but with safety equipment so kids can learn new tricks, foam pits, resin floors, that sort of thing."

Kaylene's interest perked up at the mention of foam pits. "What do you think about Woodward?" she asked Aaron.

He shrugged. He had known about the camp for a while but had never mentioned it to her, probably thinking we couldn't afford it.

"I think it's a good idea," she said.

"You do?"

"Well, can you think of a better place to practice a backflip?"

Kaylene submitted an application, but when Woodward learned Aaron was in a wheelchair, they denied it. So she called to speak with Debbie Williams.

"I don't understand why you won't accept my son's application," Kaylene said.

"We've had a few men try our camps on wheelchairs," Debbie explained. "Full-grown men, mind you. It didn't work out."

"Aaron's different," Kaylene argued. "He's an incredible athlete. He doesn't just compete with the BMXers at these competitions. He wins them. He does the same tricks they do."

"I'm sure he does," Debbie said.

"But he needs this camp. You have the right equipment for the kinds of tricks he wants to learn."

"And that would be?"

"Well, he needs the foam pit for a backflip."

Wheelz

Debbie sighed. "We had someone try a backflip on a chair not long ago."

"And?"

"It didn't work out. The rotation is impossible. He couldn't get enough height from the ramps, and he couldn't rotate quickly enough to land on all four wheels. It can't be done."

"Maybe," Kaylene said, not willing to concede the point. "I'm sure your guy was competent in a chair, and I'm not disparaging him for trying, but maybe Aaron is a stronger athlete."

Debbie tried a different angle. "You understand that it's not just the possibility of failure. Our greatest concern is your son's safety. We won't do anything to compromise on that issue."

"I'll sign waivers of liability. I can provide proof of insurance, whatever it takes to assure you that we take full responsibility for his health and safety."

"We don't have accessibility ramps," Debbie said. "We're not staffed to take care of any special needs."

"Aaron doesn't need any of that," Kaylene assured her. "All he needs is a ramp and a foam pit."

Debbie sighed again. "I'll talk to my directors. I'm not promising anything, but I'll see what I can do."

Kaylene had little hope as she hung up the phone. A few weeks later, however, Debbie called. "They've decided to let him give it a try," she said.

"Excellent," Kaylene said.

"He may have to come home early. Do you understand that?"

"Uh hm."

"We will not offer you a refund if he does."

"Fine."

"Then we look forward to welcoming him in a few weeks."

When I dropped Aaron off at the camp, people were curious. The kids and coaches stared as he rode past them to his bungalow. We knew they were wondering what this kid was doing there on a wheelchair with a full face helmet on his knee, a toolbox in his lap, and his dad following him with extra wheels and a sleeping bag. We both ate up the attention. Some of the counselors asked if he was going to ride.

In my pride I wanted to say, "Like a pro! You'll be blown away!"

Instead I nodded and said, "Yeah." They'd see soon enough.

I didn't worry about Aaron fitting in or making friends at camp. It's hard to have a sport if you're the only one doing it. But there is an advantage to being the only one: everyone likes you. None of the skaters or bikers at Woodward saw him as competition. The only place where he was a threat was at home – in Pro Park, during the Am Jams. Everyone else was genuinely interested in what he could do. So any new skate park is fun, and Wheelz has instant friends.

Aaron wanted to try a local park while we visited Park City, Utah, once. When he rode up to the park, everyone stopped. A kid in a chair is not so unusual. But this one had a helmet. He rode around the outer rim, surveyed the possibilities, and then put on his helmet. The bikers and skaters were not sure what was next. Aaron then rolled to the edge of a twelve-foot drop. He poised his front wheels over the edge. There was silence. Aaron dropped in and rolled around the bowl like a kid on a bike.

Immediately, the kids ran over and said things like "That was awesome!" Without asking, they helped him out of the bowl. Such things happened frequently. So when I left him at Woodward, I knew he would have a good time.

He practiced doing his backflip in Woodward's foam pit for a day and a half. Debbie was right; getting enough speed and a quick enough rotation was impossible -- well, almost impossible. And that wasn't the worst of it.

The foam pit was absolute torture. Being upside-down, strapped to a wheelchair in squares of foam, is suffocating. Whether or not you're claustrophobic elsewhere, you are without fail in the foam pit. The dirt, the foam dust — it is all terrible. Aaron once landed there perfectly, headfirst. Upside-down, disoriented, he couldn't get off his chair. He panicked and thrust his arms. But the chair kept coming down on him. Finally, a kid jumped in and rescued him.

Most kids can use their whole bodies -- arms and legs -- to "swim" through the foam and pull themselves out with the rope. Aaron had to use only his arms, and he had to drag his chair with him. And he did it dozens of times. But in spite of his exhaustion, it worked.

After just one day he called his mom and said he could land it in the foam pit.

"You've got to be kidding me," she said.

After he was comfortable with the rotation over the foam pit, he moved on to "the Rezy" – a resin sheet over large foam pads. It

Wheelz

wasn't as suffocating as the pit, but it was also less forgiving. Aaron crashed on it dozens of times. Then, on July 13th, 2006, at 8:57 p.m., he landed the first wheelchair backflip. He called his mom.

"Mom," he said, his voice dripping with excitement and leftover adrenaline, "I landed it for real."

"No, you didn't."

"Yes, I did."

"No, you didn't."

"Really, Mom, I did."

Kaylene thought she'd misunderstood. "You mean you landed it in the foam pit."

"No, Mom," he said, the patience beginning to ebb out of his voice, "I landed it on the rezy."

Kaylene paused as the truth sank in. "That's amazing," she said finally.

"I know! It took me, like, a minute to realize what I did. But then, when I didn't fall backwards and hit my head, I was like, 'Whoa, that's cool.'"

Aaron's next call was to me. I was driving up Tropicana after an evening class. I had just passed the Thomas and Mack Athletic Center.

"Dad," he said, "I landed a backflip."

I couldn't even picture it in my mind. And it came out of nowhere. All the way on the trip to Woodward, he had not even mentioned the backflip. I had no clue he was considering such a harebrained idea. And now he was telling me he had done something I was sure no person in the history of the world had done. I honestly didn't know what to think.

"A backflip?" I asked, and then the dadside of me kicked in. "How long have you been planning this?"

"A while," he admitted. "I was just getting bored, you know? I wanted to do something cool that had never been done before."

"Well, you did," I said. "You're right up there with..." I hesitated. Aaron's idol was Travis Pastrana, the first motocross rider to do a backflip and a double backflip. He had been singing Travis's praises for years. I caught myself because Aaron wouldn't appreciate the comparison. But Aaron was already moving on.

"It was so hard to get the rotation. It had to be so fast, and I kept underrotating. I kept getting stuck in that stupid foam pit."

I had no idea what he was talking about. "But you did it," I said, more to myself than to him.

"Yeah."

"That's so cool," I said.

His excitement was infectious. I told my friends, but it didn't sink in until he got home. I honestly couldn't picture it in my mind. Luckily, Ryan "Buzzy" Sullivan captured it on video, and Bart Jones got it on high-speed camera. When I watched it all I said was, "Wow!" All I thought was, *Nike*.

A Life of Its Own

After seeing the flip I went to Mitch Truman's house for advice. All his friends called him Moe.

"How do I contact Gatorade or Nike?" I asked. "I think a backflip in a wheelchair fits the slogan 'Just do it' pretty well."

"Don't do it," Moe said. "Don't prostitute your son."

Moe is the only guy I know who wears a bowtie. He's tall and thin everywhere, even in his face, with wire-rimmed glasses and short hair. He reminds me of every science teacher I've ever had. He once gave me a sixty-dollar bowtie. I couldn't tie it and felt dumb wearing it, so it just sits in my closet now. But Moe, that guy walks to the beat of a different drummer. I can't imagine he was ever self-conscious.

As a teenager, he put his parents through hell. He drank whatever alcohol he could get his hands on. Moe tried every illegal drug that came his way. His parents were losing him, so his dad put him to work at his trucking company, a last-ditch effort to save their son. He paid Mitch a dollar an hour and scheduled him for twelve-hour shifts. It worked. Mitch straightened up, turned his life around, and applied to go to college.

At school he was reintroduced to the religion he had all but forsaken. He served a proselyting mission in England for two years. He came home and married a girl who could tolerate his attention-deficient, 100-miles-per-hour modus operandi, and he began to look around him for ways to help anyone in need.

Moe ran his dad's trucking company. Pan Western was a large, successful delivery company in Vegas, but that didn't faze Moe. If he made money, he gave it away. When gas prices went up and the American economy went down, Moe's company was destroyed. But that didn't shorten his generous stride.

He took one of his semi-trailers and turned it into the biggest kitchen on wheels I've ever seen. It had stoves, a couple of conveyor pizza ovens, an industrial ice maker, a refrigerator, tables and chairs enough to feed an army, an ice cream machine, grills, and more. Every week he took his truck and fed some youth or Scout group.

He gave me more than a tie. I was once admiring his industrial-sized evaporative cooler. The next day he had one delivered to my home.

One time he came to where I worked and said, "Your students need grills."

Before we knew it, a huge truck was backing up into our parking lot with a 4000-dollar flat slab grill and a 4000-dollar barbecue grill. A month or two later, he delivered a 4000-dollar soft-serve ice cream machine. A while later he delivered a whipped hot chocolate machine. He also convinced a friend to donate an ice machine.

I once mentioned to him that a single mother with five children could use an evaporative cooler and offered to pay my part. He had a stand made and the cooler delivered within the month. He never let me pay anything.

I loved to argue with Moe, but regarding financial things, he had my full trust. It was obvious his heart was pure. After talking to Moe we would not commercialize our boy. We would let his career have a life of its own.

It took about two weeks for Moe's advice to prove wise. News of that backflip went global in days. One of the first people to contact us was Manuela (Manu) Zahn, the sales and marketing head of wheelchair tires for the Schwalbe Tire Company located in Germany.

Just before Aaron's flip, John and Mike Box, the owners of Colours Wheelchairs, had started corresponding with Manu. When Aaron hit his backflip, John immediately informed Manu, and she, in turn, immediately asked for Aaron to come to

Wheelz

Germany. *Mountain Bike Rider* magazine of Germany had organized a Homegrown Tour for January, and Manu wanted Aaron to join that tour.

Once Manu contacted us, she and Kaylene began making plans for Aaron's visit. She also started sending Aaron tires, which, incidentally, lowered the level of anger in our home by at least twenty percent. Before Aaron got those tires, he popped at least one tire every other week.

Wheelchair tires -- especially his -- have to be tightly secured to the rims, and they are painfully difficult to remove. Furthermore, it is easy to puncture new inner tubes when putting the tires back on. Aaron replaced his tires himself, but it was always an exercise in anger management, and one at which he often failed. He threw tools; he swore. When he repaired tires in the entry of our house, the rest of the family disappeared until the ordeal was over.

Manu's tires were wonderful because they didn't need to be replaced nearly as often! We were so thrilled that Kaylene wrote to her immediately.

Dear Manu,

We thought you might like to know that Aaron is continuing to learn new stunts. In the process, he has bent his wheelchair frame, broken a helmet, and destroyed two

Wheelz

Spinergy wheels (pulled the spokes right out of the hubs and rims). But he hasn't popped an inner tube and the tires are great. He likes the Marathon Plus tires best and would like another set because they are losing their tread. And could he get a couple more inner tubes that fit the Marathon Plus?

Thanks,
Kaylene

Manu sent five sets of tires, twelve tubes, and a cool bag as a gift for Aaron, but the best gift was her assurance that Schwalbe tires was fully prepared to sponsor Aaron and supply his tires for the rest of his career.

Schwalbe's pledge of support was just one of many instances of a growing worldwide community that began turning an interested eye in his direction. People offered to print t-shirts and stickers and to develop websites for him. Adam Roberts, a disabled artist, volunteered to create a t-shirt design and logo.

While many wrote to give, even more wrote to request something. The media wanted basically the same things: interviews, DVDs, photos, and answers. We did not know when this window of opportunity would close, so Kaylene responded to everyone's requests as if they were the last. For example, Brenda with *PVA Magazine* asked for photos and information about the "other side" of Aaron's life.

Kaylene's response offers some insight into Aaron at that time:

To Brenda at *PVA Magazine*,

I just got your message. I will send a few pictures, but we couldn't find many of him not in the skate park. His other hobbies don't lend themselves to being photographed.

We have three dogs now, counting the new puppy. I ride horses and have two, but Aaron has no interest in them. (I suppose they are pets at best to him.) Another thing that Aaron spends time doing is taking photos and making movies. He is learning to shoot and develop film the old-fashioned way and loving it. He also makes movies on our computer; he made the movie of himself at the skate parks with footage shot from his camera by friends.

He is also interested in welding and mechanical engineering. He wants to build "wicked awesome" wheelchairs someday. He also enjoys drawing. Not so much artistic but illustrating his creative ideas, and he is full of creative ideas. Basically, Aaron never sits still; he is active and creative and full of energy. He does not deal with boredom well. Being home with nothing in particular to do is a fate worse than death for him.

Aaron is funny and he keeps the family and his close friends laughing most of the time. He uses his challenges as material for jokes and resents it if people take his disability seriously or feel sorry for him. He knows that if he was able to walk he would not be as unique and therefore just one of the crowd. As it is, he definitely stands out. He told me a while ago that he can never get away with anything because everyone knows him and he is easy to pick out in a crowd.

He is a little shy in new situations, and all this has sort of taken him by surprise. Sometimes he loves all the attention, and other times he wishes it would all go back to the way it used to be. He thinks it is funny but a little embarrassing when people stop him to ask if he is the kid that did the backflip.

I am sorry we could not come up with more pictures, but I don't think about taking pictures except at holidays and vacations. The three we found are kayaking at Catalina Island, California, with his dad and brother Brian, him playing around with his guitar (he used to play a lot, but it is sort of a past dream), and Aaron with his new puppy (he named her Colours). Family pictures are hard to come by

Wheelz

around here because the kids are so spread out in age. (Two are grown and gone from home, and the youngest is only six.) Our last family picture was taken almost four years ago. Aaron looks real young and he did not want it sent.

I hope this gives you a little more material. If you need more I should be home all day tomorrow (cleaning house and getting ready for Thanksgiving). I will check my e-mail often and answer any more questions you might have.

Thanks,
Kaylene

It is amazing and more than a little hard to believe that Kaylene gave such personal and lengthy responses to all requests. And the requests never stopped.

As soon as Aaron could afford a computer, he took over making his own DVDs. He was thrilled when a video he made hit the top five on Myspace. It featured a number of his tricks, including the backflip. The video also included Bryce Howell. Bryce was best friends with Joey. Bryce also had spina bifida and used a walker. When his parents ordered him a Colours Wheelchair, Bryce's mother asked if Aaron could help him learn how to use it.

So they met at the skate park one evening. Aaron showed Bryce some tricks. Then he showed him how to get up and down curbs and a little about balance. Next, he took Bryce in the bowls and pushed him around. Aaron pushed his own chair with one hand and pushed Bryce with his other hand. Bryce put his hands out like an airplane. Later, Bryce told his mother he felt like an Eagle. She complained later to Kaylene, "Bryce never waits for us."

VIDEO 3: Shows his power slide, jumping the steps in junior high, rainbow grind, and first backflip.

http://goo.gl/G1YJ9J

Kaylene copied the first sixteen comments from Myspace. They were all kind. I'll quote only one:

> Hey I saw this video of a kid called Aaron Fotheringham in his wheelchair. I thought that this kid is an awesome inspiration, I do skateboarding myself and have learning difficulties and as a result no coordination! But this has got me buzzing and I think I'm going to dust my deck off and deal with things. Thanks Aaron you're awesome.

Of the television programs documenting his backflip, the best was a show called *HOLY @#% Bleep!* They titled his segment "Man Versus Gravity," and we watched that program as a family over and over again. Without question, what Aaron liked the most was being featured with his idol Travis Pastrana.

The show vocalized what we were all thinking: Aaron was defining a new sport. His audience could reach into the hundreds of thousands or even millions, and his potential, it seemed, was boundless. At first, we hoped we could keep up with him; we soon stopped trying.

Doing that flip on the Rezy and doing it on concrete, however, are two different things. I knew enough not to stand in his way, despite my reservations. Aaron had a place at Pro Park he thought would give him enough height. He consulted a doctor and decided to give it a try.

It was a Monday night late in July. Our neighbors, the Childs, and our family went with cameras to document the attempt. Aaron sped down a steep ramp, then pushed hard about a hundred feet to the launch, trying to pick up speed. The first few times he didn't attempt to flip. He wanted to see how much air he could get. Completing the flip would require a tight tuck and a fast rotation. After a few of those practice runs, he was ready to try.

It was the only trick – including seeing him on the MegaRamp – where I was seriously nervous. My wife was terrified. The stunt offered basically three options: land it, land on his face, or hit the back of his head. It would be easy to over- or underrotate.

On the first try, he overrotated and smashed his face (with his helmet) into the concrete. For the second try, he smacked the back of his head. He tried about ten times. A few times, he was close – but he never landed it that night. Having his friends and family there and repeatedly failing was disappointing for him. We were thrilled, however, with how close he had come.

Soon enough, though, he started landing it on a regular basis. He also crashed on a regular basis. It took about a year before landing it was more the norm. Until then, every miss was painful.

I tried to convince him that landing it on concrete once was enough. We could video it for proof. With the weight of that chair and the speed of his rotation, it was a scary thing. But I was wrong. He practiced it until he mastered it. What I didn't realize and what he almost instinctively knew was when the media came to see him – and they came every week – they wanted to see the backflip. He had to be able to show them it wasn't a one time lucky stunt.

Tour of Germany

One of the sad things about Mr. Wheelington (as Chad Kagy would one day call him) is that he doesn't care to travel. Aaron would end up seeing more of the world than most people, but it would mean little to him. When he was much older, we saw the Great Wall of China together. I was in awe of its history, let alone its grandeur. It is, after all, one of the Seven Wonders of the World. Wheelz was simply wondering how wide it was and if there was a good place to jump it.

So a trip to Germany at age fifteen meant nothing to him but that he would have to endure a long flight in cramped seating. He also wasn't thrilled about all the interviews he would have to do. He was still that shy kid who would just as soon roll away as carry on a conversation with a stranger--especially a stranger with a camera. But he knew that he had a sponsor to uphold and a sport to promote.

His mom, on the other hand, was thrilled to see Germany, although she was keenly aware that those cameras would turn, as they invariably did, on her.

Their contact in Germany, Manu was a tall, attractive blonde who was extremely upbeat, prone to hospitality, and one of Aaron's first and lifelong fans. Before she even met us, she treated us like family and Aaron like a younger brother. Aaron's backflip was the initial spark for her marketing genius. She hired a press agent to contact news stations and other media outlets for every town on their itinerary. As a result, nearly every German TV station, newspaper, and radio station was present at the competitions. They all interviewed Wheelz. It was impossible to turn on the television and not see him. Every night he and his mom would watch the local news. The anchors would say something unintelligible in German and then they would hear "Aaron Fotheringham" and "Hardcore Sitting." That's all Aaron wanted to hear. The word was getting out. Then they invariably showed one of the videos his press agent had given them.

One of Manu's preliminary emails had advised Aaron not to worry about bringing extra tires: "We've got millions." When he got to Germany, Manu commissioned Thomas Schmiking, an engineer like Mike Box, to design Aaron some wheels. They held up like nothing before. More than supplying wheels, Manu treated her American guests well. Because of that, Aaron was willing to do whatever she asked. Although he preferred to ride, he played his part when the cameras were on.

In actuality, he really had to grow into that part. Their first stop was Prague in the Czech Republic. There was one reporter. From then on Aaron was swarmed by the media at every stop. At first he was shy and intimidated. He soon became irritated by their audacity. They had no problem questioning him with cameras in his face while he was trying to eat lunch. When he realized they weren't going away, he figured that he might as well enjoy them, and so he did.

He spoke to schools. He tried snow and water skiing, and did some shopping. The media was always there. Aaron soon learned to relax and enjoy all the attention. He had no way of knowing this was to be his life for years. He grew up quickly in Germany.

When the tour was over, the press agent and Manu seemed pleased with all of the exposure Schwalbe received. Aaron and Kaylene were tired. They were ready to go home--until Manu got one last media request. It was for Aaron to appear on the *Stefan Raab show*. Stefan Raab is Germany's Jay Leno. Both Schwalbe and the press agent were thrilled, and all Aaron had to do was wear a Schwalbe shirt.

It was more publicity than anyone could have hoped for, but it was also more stress. With the local stations Aaron could answer questions and just talk until they got what they wanted. Back in their studios they would cut and splice and make him look good. Stefan Raab was different. It was live and national.

The show had small ramps built for him. When Aaron came rolling out, his music blared throughout the studio. He did some tricks on the ramps, then bounced up the stairs to talk to Mr. Raab, who, luckily, spoke great English. He asked the standard questions and showed one of his videos, but unlike all of the other times, Aaron wasn't finished.

He still had to do something worthwhile on the show. Stefan Raab wanted a performance—hence the ramps -- but they were only about three feet high, with nothing to launch from. After the video and interview, Aaron dropped down those steps and played around on the ramps again. He did everything he could think of. He sat on the front of his seat and rolled down the ramp. He spun a 360 on one wheel. He jumped off the side. . He did a good job with what he had to work with. It wasn't much compared to his videos, though. It wasn't anywhere close to a backflip.

Aaron felt himself getting nervous. Under different circumstances, the flutter of excitement in his stomach might have meant he was about to try something new -- something that could just as easily land him in the emergency room as set a world record. But this was different. He had to impress a live audience and hundreds of thousands of viewers on those dinky ramps.

But in the end, Stefan Raab was willing to do his part. He motioned for his staff to bring out a wheelchair, then jumped onto it and flexed his arms. The audience loved his bravado. Then he tried to go up the ramp. He went up about a foot and realized it took a lot more strength than he had supposed. He backed up for a longer run and tried again. He got no further. On the third attempt he hit the ramp and fell out of his chair onto his knees.

Wheelz

Aaron had made it look so easy. The audience and Stefan now knew better.

Aaron sat on the side watching. He was unmindful that his two front wheels were, as usual, floating off the ground. Raab tried to do the same. He lifted his wheels up about two inches. They fell immediately to the floor as if they were made of lead. He saw no value in trying again.

When Aaron first came out on the show, he'd had to get up a two-tiered stage. The first was about ten inches high; the second was about five. With one thrust he climbed the first tier like he was rolling over a tiny speed bump. He then rode about seven feet to reach the second platform. He lifted one wheel and then the next in a rocking motion and was up in a simple one-two stride. It was no big deal. I assume few gave it any thought. I'm sure other kids on chairs climb stairs that way. I just have never seen it. What I have seen is people get out of their chairs and drag them up.

Most people on wheelchairs don't like stairs. BMXers and skateboarders love stairs, so Aaron has always loved them. Even as a baby stairs were a toy. Like the rainbow grind, he was not satisfied until he owned them. Soon he was flying over them or bouncing down them. When the stairs are narrow he turns his chair backwards, grabs the hand rail, and rides down backwards.

Had Stefan Raab noticed it, he would have realized lifting two wheels is just a beginning of controlling a wheelchair. But he didn't notice it. If Aaron had had to drag himself up and across those platforms, he would have brought attention to the fact that his legs don't work. Instead he looked like a kid on a bike hopping curbs. He did not crawl up to be interviewed by Mr. Raab. He rode up.

Stefan asked Aaron about his suspension. Aaron lifted three wheels off the ground, balanced on one for a few moments, then bounced up and down about three inches high to show his shock compress.

Aaron did a 360 on one wheel again, suggesting Stefan Raab give it a try. Mr. Raab couldn't get a back wheel off the ground. Instead, he just spun in circles, all four wheels glued to the floor. He tried again and got a back wheel up for about two seconds. The crowd cheered. Aaron's pulse slowed. He didn't have to do a backflip on the show -- he just had to be himself.

I did not begrudge Aaron or Kaylene the trip to Germany. They had worked hard to get there and worked hard while they were there. But I didn't like her being gone for so long.

When they finally returned, I said, "Tell me this was worth it."

She said, "All I need to do is tell you one story. Aaron's first exhibition was in Prague. Only one news crew showed up. A young man saw the story that night. He had recently been in a car accident that had left him paralyzed from the waist down. When he heard Aaron would next be in Wuppertal, he went to great lengths to get out of rehab to meet him. At Wuppertal, Aaron was swarmed with the media. When Manu found the young man, she pulled Aaron away from the media, who then turned their attention to the young man. They asked him what he thought about Aaron.

He said, 'Now I know my life isn't over.'"

That was all I needed to hear.

Then Kaylene said, "We're going back next year."

Hardcore Sitting

Long before reporters were calling him the pioneer of a new sport, before he competed in his first Am Jam, Aaron knew he was inventing a sport. That's why he went to great efforts to come up with a name. When he did he had his mom get Hardcore Sitting trademarked.

In an interview with ESPN Joe Wichert said,
"The kid, not only the way he rides the park, but when you talk to him, he's positive, polite, level-headed.... It's great to see someone like Aaron creating a whole new sport."

Aaron always took a sketchpad and pencils to church to work on HCS lettering and logo. I glanced over every week and saw his designs improve. He instinctively knew the sport had to be as independent as Skateboarders were from BMXers. Hardcore Sitting had to be a sport on its own. He deeply disliked when anyone called it Wheelchair Skateboarding. It was Hardcore Sitting.

When he was in Germany he wasn't promoting himself. Every news station included Hardcore Sitting with his name.

When he appeared on *The Stefan Raab Show* he wore a Schwalbe shirt that had "Hardcore Sitting" in bold white letters on his right sleeve.

On that show Stefan Raab asked, "When did you start doing tricks with the wheelchair?"

"I started Hardcore Sitting when I was nine."

Stefan responded, "All right, he named it Hardcore Sitting. Okay? Ha, ha."

Aaron's immediate goals were learning new tricks, winning his next Am Jam competition, and riding a MegaRamp, but undergirding all of this he wanted some competition in a sport he knew would grow.

The media blitz that began with a backflip never ended.

Aaron let his mom worry about that. He continued to participate in Am Jam Competitions whenever he had the chance. He won two second-place trophies and two third-place trophies in the BMX Intermediate Competitions the year before. When he got home from Germany in time for the 2007 February Am Jam, he took third. And while he had been an international sensation in Europe, I really believe those competitions were equally as -- if not more -- important to him than all the fuss surrounding that tour.

As long as he could ride, it was all the same to him. So while his parents and the other adults wasted time wondering how he would handle the press and pressure, he was busy doing exactly the opposite. Indeed, his patience and politeness when confronted with yet another interview exceeded everyone's expectations. And there was no better testament to his ability to handle the media than when Schwalbe asked him to become an official representative. When he agreed, they sent a contract providing him with unlimited supplies and a monthly stipend. The money was nice. The vote of confidence was wonderful.

Kaylene, however, ended up with a job she never applied for, and it soon became much bigger than she'd anticipated. After Germany, the media attention that had seemed like a little campfire turned into a raging inferno. Denmark, Sweden, England, France, Chile, Japan, Korea -- everybody wanted a piece of him. New Zealand and Canada wanted to include articles on him in school books. Nearly everyone requested interviews. Many wanted to buy footage. Kaylene became an extreme sports agent with no experience.

She wrote to John Box and Mike Jakie of Woodward for advice on how to navigate the business world. At the same time, she corresponded continually with lawyers to trademark Aaron's logo and Hardcore Sitting.

She spent much of her time trying to find an agent for Aaron, but nobody wanted to represent him. He was a unicorn, and they didn't know any more than she did about what to do with him.

On January 19th, 2007, only a couple weeks after the Homegrown Tour, she wrote to John Box,

> We are desperate for an international sports agent now. I cannot keep track of all this and still do my job at home. We have been given a reference for one out of Switzerland and I just don't know how to know if this person will be honest and good for Aaron. Overwhelmed is not a big enough word right now.
>
> Please let me know your thoughts on all this and any advice you might have. Thanks for being there from the start.
>
> Kaylene and Aaron

John wrote back, "Trust your gut."

Germany had shown Kaylene what a good agent could do. It only took two short weeks for Aaron to become a household name in that country. But agents in America couldn't see any money in it, and neither could we.

> She wrote to Manu
>
> A shock company has contacted us and they want to design a shock for Hardcore Sitting. Georgia Tech University has contacted us because they want to design a lighter wheelchair. It is all very exciting, and more than a little overwhelming. We are learning and growing and maybe someday we will understand it all.

On top of all that, Aaron kept breaking things. Kaylene was in constant contact with Mike to request new chairs. She corresponded with Manu daily for advice and help with wheels. The best she had seen were out of Germany, but Aaron broke them much faster than anyone in Germany could ship them.

Six Six One sponsored Aaron in equipment like helmets and pads. They were supportive but sometimes slow to respond. When Troy Lee Designs offered to take over the sponsorship, Kaylene didn't know what to do. She turned to Mike Jackie of Woodward, who told her that it wasn't cool for athletes to bounce between sponsors. She let Six Six One know she had offers. They said they wanted to keep him. She remained loyal to them and they took care of Aaron until years later, when he switched to Troy Lee. She also dealt extensively with FoxShox for shocks and Frog Legs for his front suspension.

Learning the ins and outs of sponsorship kept her on her toes. She managed his growing schedule of interviews and competitions and tried to sort through the confusion to find the best avenues for his talent. And while Kaylene was running herself ragged, Aaron wanted nothing to do with any of it. He was willing to be interviewed. He was kind to anyone who came for a story. He went as a guest to various camps and demos if he could fit it into his schedule, but if he needed an axle, he called his mom.

At the end of April 2007, Las Vegas dedicated their largest skate park. Joe invited Aaron to be one of the riders on the opening day. Wheelz cared little for the million-dollar park, but he was interested in the stairs. They were five feet high and he needed to cover about sixteen feet to clear them. He cleared them and was done with that park.

The next day he landed three backflips in an Am Jam competition. It wasn't enough to bring home a trophy, but he hardly cared. As much as he loved Am Jam competitions, he really didn't need any more trophies. And he still felt a little bad that his friends lost to a kid on a wheelchair. He repeatedly asked the judges to ignore him. He merely wanted to ride. A crowd watching was all he needed.

On September 22nd, 2007, Aaron took First Place BMX at Intermediate Am Jam. With his schedule, Aaron could no longer attend public school.

The media barrage was overwhelming, but it wasn't all negative. Kaylene loved getting inquiries from ABC, NBC, MTV, *The Bonnie Hunt Show*, *The Ellen DeGeneres Show*, *Maury*, the Associated Press, and Nike.

Nike

On November 28th, 2007, I got a call from Kaylene. "You'll never guess who just called – Nike! They want Aaron to audition for a commercial tomorrow."

We had mixed emotions--joy and elation. But we were concerned. Nike, in our view, is as high as you can go. We had always dreamt of that, but this was too early, too fast. Where would Aaron go from there? He was fairly philosophical about the whole thing. Sure, he would like to do a commercial. He would like the money. But he didn't wear Nikes.

The Nike marketing group arranged for a video link audition at a local Kinko's. They sent Aaron a script they wanted him to read in the interview. It was accompanied with a letter of confidentiality requiring we say nothing about the contents of the commercial.

The link to the audition was with two men in Oregon and one in Argentina. All we knew about them was they represented Nike. Aaron was nervous, and the link made it difficult. There was a slight delay in the video feed. It all felt unnatural. Aaron did fine, but in real life, he would have done much better. It usually takes a few minutes for him to forget the cameras. When he does and when he can be himself, it is a whole different experience.

A few weeks later, the group called and said they presented the idea to Nike and Nike decided to go in a different direction. We were disappointed but not too much. Aaron went to the skate park.

Years later, Aaron was in a couple Nike commercials. They featured a bunch of people performing amazing stunts. Aaron was one of them, doing his backflip. It was neat and he can always claim he was in a Nike commercial, but we were wrong. It was not as high as he could go; that would be a ramp in Brazil. The media coverage he got for that jump did indeed surpass any Nike commercial. The truth is that every step in his career seemed to be as far as he could go. Every couple of weeks we realized we were wrong.

At one point in that initial Nike interview, they asked, "What's your next trick?"

Aaron responded, "You'll have to sign a letter of confidentiality before I tell you."

They laughed and said, "Fair enough."

For that brief moment they found Aaron. They should have signed that letter – because his next trick would rival the backflip.

A Handplant

"He's constantly needing things in equipment," says John Box, [who] figures it costs $20,000 a year to keep Fotheringham on wheels. "I've been in a chair 25 years," says Box, who was injured in a motorcycle crash. "I've done everything – hockey, tennis, football, rugby, basketball, and skydiving. But there's no one doing what Aaron does from the extreme level. It makes you want to get off the couch, turn off the remote and do something with your life." (March 15th, 2007, Associated Press)

"What do you mean, tacoed?" I asked.

Aaron explained, "It's when you bend your rims so your wheels look like a taco shell."

All of a sudden, he was tacoing wheels every day. To replace a wheel Kaylene would call Colours and request a hub. They would send it to DT Swiss in Colorado. They added spokes and a rim then sent it back to Colours. Colours would then connect the outer handrail and ship it to our house.

Kaylene really wanted Spinergy. They were not as strong as DT Swiss, but they were pretty good and they made wheelchair wheels. They were also expensive and told her, "We don't sponsor

Wheelz

kids in wheelchairs." She pestered them. Aaron needed them so badly she couldn't give up. But it was without success.

She also called Colours every day, trying to describe another broken part to them. She requested boxes of axels. He bent dozens of them. We weren't sure what was going on, but he was destroying chairs and wheels and axels like never before.

I eventually learned that Aaron was working on a handplant. The idea was for him to launch up the ramp and, instead of flying to the platform, plant his hand at the top of the ramp and turn back down the ramp in mid-air. It required much more timing and finesse than the backflip. The tuck and the turn to get the wheels in a position to head back down without hitting the coping was incredibly difficult.

Until he mastered a handplant he had to turn before he came to the coping. It was a simple U-turn that looked like a simple U-turn. The handplant allowed him to maintain or even increase his speed. It was a powerful return thrusting him back down the way he came up.

Smacking his chair on the edge of the box with tremendous force, he immediately bent something. If he landed at the wrong angle, his wheels would taco.

Kaylene tried to convince him to stop. She was tired of getting calls from him after only a few minutes at the park: "You need to come get me. I ruined another wheel." But Aaron didn't stop.

Despite the damage to the chair, it was torture to his body. He was jumping two feet above the box then landing on his face with a 25-pound chair strapped to his back. He had been doing that for months before that Nike interview.

Outside Magazine got the first look at the handplant. They had him repeat it dozens of times to get the shot they wanted. I'm not sure he landed it squarely that day, but they eventually got the photo. Soon after their visit he could land it routinely.

I believe someone will do a backflip on a wheelchair in the future. I believe they'll do tricks Aaron never thought of. We hope they do. But a handplant – if someone does that, I'll be impressed.

ESPN Comes to Town

Just amazing – he's good. This is all kids need to see, by the way. If you need motivation to succeed, take a look at Aaron. Wow, he's amazing. Chris Cuomo, (2/13/2008, *ABC News, Good Morning America*).

The first week of December 2007, ESPN came to town to interview Wheelz. They reserved Pro Park with the city. Aaron spent the day with them. The segment aired the next week. It only lasted one minute and eight seconds, but it was pretty good.

A week or so later, the folks at ESPN wanted to do a larger documentary. They came to Vegas again. They interviewed us. It turned out to be a four-minute work of art. What follows are just a few quotes.

Tom Rinaldi asked Aaron, "How would you define spina bifida?"

Aaron: "A great opportunity."

Tom asked Aaron if there was anything he wanted?
"Yeah some competition."

Joe Wichert said "I was blown away. I was completely – I saw this little kid, and he's the same age as my son, and I couldn't believe the drive and the determination that he had in his eyes to do this."

Wheelz

My wife, referring to a second trip to Germany, said, "Aaron was interviewed by reporters and everything, and it was — it was kind of a whirlwind opportunity, and this little boy who can't speak any English because we're in Germany, but just a little bit of English, he comes up to me. I don't know that he knew that I was Aaron's mother. He holds up this poster and hugs it to his chest and he says, 'Mein Aaron autograph! Mein Aaron autograph!' And I remember I was just sitting there and bawling, thinking, *Wow — that's my kid*"

But the best part of the segment was with little Zachary Puddy. I will quote it entirely.

Tom Rinoldi: "At sixteen, known by all his friends as 'Wheelz,' Aaron seems just another teenager dropping and carving and spinning. But to four-year-old Zachary, in a wheelchair as a result of a stroke he suffered three years ago, Aaron is magical."

Showing Aaron and Zach at the top of a ramp, Aaron said: "You go first."

Zachery: "No — you."

Aaron: "No — you. I'll help you, then I'll go."

Tom: "After seeing Aaron's backflip, Linda Puddy reached out to him and traveled from Seattle to Vegas so her son could meet Aaron in person. The connection was immediate."

They ride. Zachary giggles.

Linda : "He's a hero. He's a hero. He thinks Aaron flies. I hope the other kids like Zachary can find that, too, because I didn't know what to do with him until we saw Aaron. And then I knew. That gives us a direction to go."

Aaron: "Just seeing their faces watching me makes me want to help them. Even if they don't go to the park, I just want to be able to help them live a better life."

VIDEO 4: The following link is the Breaking Barriers video
http://goo.gl/khHc9T

A few days after the story aired, the director called and said, "We have never had such a positive response." What follows are two of the hundreds of comments they got in a two-day period on the ESPN site.

Wheelz

"I'm speechless…almost. Like many before me have said, this kid IS the breakthrough athlete of the year NO DOUBT! But more importantly, an inspiration to everyone, handicapped or not. This just shows you that any kind of handicap is only in your head. Everyone should follow their heart and not let anything get in your way. I'd rather hear about these kinds of stories than the overwhelming and endless coverage that we give to the Michael Vicks, Roger Clemenses, and Barry Bonds of the world."

"This is one of the most inspiring stories I've ever seen on ESPN. Aaron is a true role model . . . Aaron's reaching out to other children to show them that they can do all the things that their friends are doing will make a huge impact on everyone's lives. I love seeing these stories on ESPN; it truly is what sports are all about."

Partly because of that ESPN coverage with Zachary and partly because of the favorable recognition Aaron brought Las Vegas, on March 5th, 2008, the city council gave him a Medal of Honor.

ABC News and *Good Morning America* aired a slightly shorter version of the ESPN story. Such coverage seriously fanned the fire. If Kaylene thought she was overwhelmed earlier, she had no idea how bad it could get. She was now getting requests from England, France, all over Europe, Korea, China, Guatemala, and too many more to mention. On top of it all, she had been

Wheelz

corresponding with the Guinness World Record people. In a way, she was pouring gas on the flame herself. She hadn't seen anything yet.

Secret Millionaire

One day in 2008 Kaylene got a call. "We're doing a new TV show and would like to include Aaron in one of our episodes. It's sort of a spinoff of *Extreme Makeover: Home Edition.* We're doing it in Vegas and want to showcase some of the city's interesting personalities."

Kaylene asked Aaron if he was interested. "I'm so through with all this. Tell them no."

Kaylene said, "You don't know what this may lead to."

"All these interviews, all these documentaries, I know they're making money off me and nobody pays me anything. I just want to ride. Tell them no."

"It gets your name out there. It promotes your cause."

He rolled out of her study, backhanding our cabinet door with his fist. A few minutes later he rolled back in. "Tell them I'll do it for a hundred bucks."

Kaylene called the lady. "He says he'll do the interview for a hundred dollars."

After a long pause the lady said, "Well, I guess, I'm not sure, we never, I'll need to check."

"It's just he gets so many requests he thinks he ought to make something on documentaries. If that's not what you do, we understand."

The lady said, "I'll check with my bosses." Then she called back and said, "They said okay."

The day of the interview Greg Haerr and his brother Paul drove up to Pro Park in a faded blue junker. A crew set up their cameras. Greg started asking the same old questions:

"How long have you been doing this? How did you start? Have you ever walked?"

"Na, spina bifida, birth defect."

"What's your best trick?"

"Backflip."

"Can we see it?"

"Sure."

Aaron strapped on his helmet and hit the flip.

"That was awesome !" Greg and Paul slapped his hand. "Do you have any goals besides doing this?"

"I want to promote this sport I call Hardcore Sitting. I want kids to know they're not limited by a wheelchair. And I'd like to make wheelchairs so they can do this."

"Do you have any things you say, or mantras or philosophies?"

"I don't think of the chair as anything bad. It sucks for you, you have to walk! I can sit down everywhere I go and ride."

Away from Aaron, Greg said to the camera, "I was inspired by Aaron. I think just one of his offhand comments, which was 'Hey, look, I'm the one with wheels, you guys gotta walk.' You know, it's just that kind of a I'm-going-to-move-forward-regardless-of-what-you're-doing attitude that I like."

Despite Aaron's rants at home, he was flattered by reporters showing up. He enjoyed the attention. He always responded politely. But a few days later that lady called again. "Would it be possible to meet with you and Aaron at the park on Friday? Greg and Paul would like to say goodbye."

Aaron told his mom, "No, I'm done with this. They asked for an interview. I gave them that. I've got other things to do."

Kaylene said, "We fulfill our obligations."

He stormed down the hall. "Tell them no!" A few minutes later he rolled back into her room. "What time do they want me?"

When they got to the park, they didn't know what to think. There were many more cameras, lights, and people. They told Aaron and Kaylene where to stand. Then Greg drove up in a limousine. He was dressed like he was rich. They still didn't know what to think.

Greg crouched down to Aaron's eye level and said, "I need to apologize to you. I lied. We're not doing a documentary. I'm a multimillionaire and I want to help you reach your dream." He handed Aaron a check for 20,000 dollars.

Aaron said, "Wow, man, that's so cool." He shook Greg's hand. "This is going to help me help those kids."

Kaylene was confused. She had no clue what the money was for, what kids Aaron was talking about. She didn't know how they wanted her to respond. Was she supposed to jump for joy or cry? She was not good at pretending either way. Then they pulled out two large, wrapped boxes. In one was a welding mask. In the other was an arc welder.

Wheelz

When my wife saw that, it all made sense. They wanted to help Aaron build chairs for people. She started to cry.

After they stopped filming Kaylene could be herself. "Thank you, thank you, this is so kind. I can't believe this." She hugged Greg.

Aaron put his arm around Greg's neck. "When my business is a success, this will come back to you."

For the next forty minutes it was a whirlwind of signing releases, giving the fake check back, setting up how he would actually receive the money, and getting the welder into the car.

The producers told them the show had not yet been sold. They said they would keep in touch and let us know if it was and when it would be aired. Until then they were not to tell anybody about it. We were excited when Fox ended up buying it.

I then got another call from Kaylene that began like so many others: "You won't believe what just happened."

About two months later, they wanted to come and film Aaron again. They wanted to see his progress towards his dream. A good friend of the family, Tim Melton, had given Aaron welding lessons. Aaron had a few metal sculptures around the yard. He had also gone to California and worked with Mike Box for a week to see how chairs were made.

When the film crew came to our house, they were a little disappointed. We are not wealthy, but we have a nice house and a beautiful backyard. I think the crew wanted a little more destitution. It would have made for a better story.

My wife said, "We never said we were poor. But let me be really clear: there is no way we could afford to have Aaron pursue his dream."

Greg was kind on camera. But he was much kinder off-camera. He seemed genuinely desirous for Aaron to reach his goals. He offered anything that would help. He kept in touch. Aaron has become a good welder. He welds bumpers and other things for his trucks. He welds for his friends.

Years later, Aaron and I were in Salt Lake City. Aaron wanted to say "Hi" to Greg. He called and said we were in town. Greg insisted we take a ride in his helicopter. That was one of the funnest things I've done in my life.

I told Kaylene, "It feels like you've died and are floating around like an angel anywhere you want to go." She was extremely jealous. I've been to Germany once; she's gone about five times with our boy. But that doesn't seem to matter: She still doesn't like it when I mention that ride. I bring it up all of the time.

Stuntman

June 2008, at the Am Jam competition, Aaron took third place BMX Intermediate class.

In July of 2008 Aaron was invited to attend a week-long camp for disabled children. After the camp, Lee Williamson, the director, wrote the following:

> July 12th, 2008
>
> Wheelz,
>
> I have to say, you are awesome . . . The skating part, dude, you're the man. I love that you are changing the way others view peeps in wheelchairs and the sports they play. This world needs more rock stars like you. The kids have been talking about you ever since you left.
>
> A quick story for you: Finess, she has CP and can't see that well, so she's leaving the skate park and usually has help getting in and out of the van. Well, she says, "Wait, let me do it," and gets in the van by herself. One of the counselors asks her, "What made you want to do it by yourself?" She said after watching "Wheelz" do it, she had to try and do it herself.
>
> Wheelz

I hope that you know that you're a role model not just to the youth around us, but you're a pioneer to the disabled community, changing the path for others to follow. It takes guts and determination and you have that.

I loved how you could play rugby, basketball, and soccer at the high levels and then turn it down to accommodate the younger kids' levels. I hope you enjoy the video, picture, and award the kids made for you.

This letter of thank you isn't just from me, it's from our entire staff and athletes. We all enjoyed you being a part of camp and hope that you will come next year as well. "Big jobs usually go to the men who prove their ability to outgrow small ones, and ability will never catch up with the demand for it." Aaron, I look forward to skating with you again. Dude, you're opening doors.

Sincerely,
Lee Williamson
Instructor Coordinator
Dominique Pacolba & Adam Elix
Camp Directors, Far West Wheelchair Sports

A number of the doors Aaron opened were for himself. If someone had told us when Mop was dragging his legs around our

Wheelz

kitchen floors that he would someday be paid to be a stuntman, we would not have believed it.

The producers of the TV series *Glee* wanted to do an episode wherein Artie was playing on his wheelchair as he went down the school hall. They called Aaron.

Aaron and his mom were flown to California, put up in an extremely nice hotel, and driven to the set. They enjoyed seeing all the actors. They were shown the different sets. The teacher's lounge set had dirty coffee cups in a sink, a popcorn machine, books lying open; it all looked so real. Seeing how the show is filmed was also fun. Aaron bounced around on his chair while they filmed him at different angles. When the episode came out, it showed Artie doing a few spins with a few shots of his wheels bouncing up and down. Aaron was paid upfront a good amount, and every time that episode plays he gets a check in the mail. He did so little.

When he gets those checks we always say the same thing: "I wonder what the real actors make?"

Later in July of 2008 Aaron got a real stunt job in Germany. Manu was contacted by Stubenstrassea, a movie production team. They were remaking a favorite German movie called *Vorstadtkrokodile* (*Suburban Gators* or *Crocodiles of the Suburbs*). One of the characters is on a *rollstuhl* (wheelchair). At one point, he gets chased down

Wheelz

two streets through a busy shopping district by bad guys on motorcycles. They wanted Aaron to do that scene.

I was tired of being left at home, so this time, I went to Düsseldorf with Kaylene and Aaron. I volunteered to pay my own way, so I sat alone in coach; Aaron's hips make cramped seating on long trips painful, so he usually requests business class. The plane was empty. I stretched out on five seats and enjoyed the ride.

In our hotel in Düsseldorf, we got a call from the production team informing us that they were sending a driver. He took us to the top of a small side street that led down to a street with stores on both sides. The stores were like any modern mall. There was a German bakery, a Subway sandwich shop, a McDonalds, and all kinds of clothing stores. Its decor was all modern, but the gray paver streets offered an old European feel. We met the director and his crew. They were kind, and most of them spoke English well.

We stood at the top of the first street as Christian, our director, said to Aaron, "The scene will start here. We want you to roll down and turn right on that street."

Aaron said, "Like this?"

He rolled down the street and picked up good speed. About ten feet before the intersection, he lifted three wheels off the ground. On his one back wheel, he arched the turn and went about ten feet down the other street before he came down on all fours. Christian turned to his assistant and said, "This is going to be good!"

I turned to Kaylene and said, "This is going to be fun!"

Before the trip, Kaylene and Aaron consulted with Stuart Wilson, a professional stuntman. Stuart doubles for Bruce Willis. Kaylene says he looks like him. He told Aaron to call the shots and not let anyone push him beyond his skill or energy level. Aaron required that a helmet be used in the shoot. The director was fine with that. It made it easier for him to look like the actor. They wanted Aaron to fly over a six-foot planter onto flat ground.

Aaron said, "No."

He needed at least a small ramp to land on. He spent the remainder of the first day discussing with the contractors the length and angles of the takeoff and landing ramps.

The day before the shoot, we went to test the ramps. The street was fairly steep downhill. It was perfect for the kind of speed Aaron needed for the six-foot gap. They secured the ramps to the concrete. Aaron put on his helmet. That caught the attention of

Wheelz

the passing crowd. They stopped to watch. Aaron went up the street, then down to the launch. He sped up the ramp and stopped with his two front wheels suspended over the edge of the gap. There, he paused to survey how he'd land and take in all the attention. He then rolled backwards down the ramp and up the hill to do it all again.

Most people can stand on a line and jump to another line. We can feel how much to push off the ground to land on the spot we aim at. Bikers and boarders and Aaron can feel what it takes to make a jump..

There is this jump I wanted Aaron to do for years. It is called "the step down." It has a two-foot protruding edge halfway down a ten-foot bowl. If he caught any part of that edge, it would bounce him facefirst to the bottom of the bowl. If he jumped out too far, he would drop ten feet onto the flat surface. Too short or too long, he would be seriously injured.

The handplant and backflip had taken a hundred crashes. The step-down wouldn't allow for one, so Aaron wisely waited until he could feel it.

I was there the evening he tried it. I had no doubt he could do it and neither did he, but it was too serious not to be scary. He sat on the ledge for the longest time. All the kids in the skate park sat on the edge of the bowl to watch. I sat on the opposite edge with

Wheelz

Aaron's camera. No matter what, it was going to be great footage. He rolled back about two feet. Then he lunged forward. He missed the edge of the step by about four inches and landed perfectly in the middle of the lower ramp. Everyone cheered. I told him I had forgotten to push record. He laughed. He was pumped. He did it a few more times to own it.

So the six-foot jump over the planter was merely fun. After a few practices up the launch, he said he was ready. He sped down the sidewalk, hit the launch squarely, flew over the planter, and landed in the middle of the down ramp into the street. The crowd enjoyed the show. Aaron enjoyed the crowd.

The day of the shoot was long but interesting. If they could get a minute for the movie in one day, it was considered a good day. They had to get from the top of the hill to the intersection at the bottom of the strip mall because they only had that street reserved for one day. The scene began with the star on a wheelchair arguing with a couple rough-looking guys on motocross bikes. At one point he picked up a watermelon and threw it at one of them.

They were shocked by his audacity, which gave him a head start to get away. He headed down the first street, grabbed a helmet some guy was carrying, and put it on. The guy protested, but to no avail.

Aaron took over from there. He sped down the street and turned onto the second street on one wheel like he had a few days before.

Wheelz

After the turn his first obstacle was a crowd of shoppers walking down the middle of the street. Aaron slalomed through them like a skier. That scene took dozens of retakes. Each time, Aaron ran the same course, but it was hard for the cameraman to get the right shot. He had a contraption strapped to his back that held a mechanical arm that came up and forward with a large camera on the front. He had to follow Aaron on a skateboard looking through that camera. That was the real stunt that day.

The day before the shoot, some of the crew told me they planned on using professional stuntmen for the intersection and final crash scenes. I showed them a video of Aaron on my iPod that included a number of crash scenes.

One of those scenes was of Aaron trying to clear the step down from the side of the bowl. He couldn't get enough speed to make it all the way across. It was a horrendous crash. I told them Aaron would face nothing like that in the intersection or crash scene. The stuntmen were impressed but said for insurance reasons they didn't have a choice. I didn't push the issue.

It was the multiple takes through all those shoppers that changed their minds. To accommodate the cameraman on the skateboard, Aaron made sure to run the same course every time. Aaron's undeviating runs so impressed the stunt people that they told the director Aaron should do the intersection. They told us the stunt needed perfect precision. With cars moving in both directions in real time and a chair swerving to miss them, there was little room for error. After watching Aaron repeat his takes, they realized none of their people could control a chair like he could. That was one the greatest compliments Aaron has ever received.

After he cleared the shoppers he needed more speed. The bikers were gaining on him. Luckily, his wheelchair was equipped with rocket boosters.

Aaron's next obstacle was a group of Hare Krishnas dressed in orange robes playing guitars and tambourines. He shot through them as they parted like a jacket unzipping.

He then was detoured by a bunch of old people crossing the street on scooters. That forced him to the sidewalk.

To get up the curb he lifted three wheels out of the way and road up the curb on his back wheel at a downward angle. Had there been an up ramp, he could not have gone up more smoothly.

A couple with a baby carriage forced him towards the planter. He jumped the planter like he'd practiced a few days before. He was upset that they were happy with the first take.

Back on the street, he headed towards the intersection. All these scenes were interspersed with shots of the star. They had him on a

Wheelz

trailer pulled with a truck, with a camera in his face. They pulled him through the same courses to splice him into the movie.

The last scene for the day was the intersection. The sun was going down and they didn't have access to the intersection the next day. It had to be done quickly and it had to be done right.

The bikers were gaining on him. The light was red. The star had no choice but to keep going. Cars were coming fast in both directions. Aaron maneuvered through them like a skater swerving around people at a roller rink. All he had to do was turn away from the cars coming at him. His downhill speed made it easy to swerve quickly. He snaked through them with ease. It was a cool-looking scene. They were satisfied with the first take.

The next day was a continuation down the street, but it was no longer the shopping district. The sidewalk was more like a plaza. Wide steps led up to a huge building.

Aaron was to start at the intersection and go as fast as he could. He was to ride up a ramp, over a gap, and land on an arcade table covered with toy prizes and stuffed animals.

They put the ramp next to the table. Aaron made one run to see how far they could make the gap. They figured about three feet wide. As they arranged the ramp and table, we sat on the steps and watched. We were surprised to see that on this day they had

Wheelz

paramedics. He was to fly off the other end of the table, which was nothing. He was to bounce down some stairs, which was nothing. We appreciated their concern but it was nothing compared to a regular day at the park.

He practiced the gap a few times. Then it started to rain. We returned to Düsseldorf and waited for three days.

Düsseldorf has beautiful parks. Kaylene and I walked to and through them all. We had nothing else to do. Downtown Düsseldorf sits next to the river Rhine. It is a quaint restaurant and shopping district with a beautiful view. In the summer evenings, the locals like to sit on the steps that descend to the Rhine and watch the sunset. There are about twenty steps, about eighty feet wide. A hundred people can sit on those steps. The people there that evening offered a great audience for a kid about to go down on a rollstuhl.

They had a ramp, but what fun would that have been? Aaron dropped down each step with ease on his back wheels. He did it slowly—methodically. The crowd stared in shock. That's what he wanted.

At the bottom of the steps is a wide walkway that meanders along the side of the river. Right next to a bridge sat two blue biker ramps facing each other. They were about eight feet high and separated by about ten feet. A biker could drop down one ramp

Wheelz

and go up the other. I thought it too perfect that they had those ramps there for my boy because there was nothing else in Düsseldorf for him to do. The German bikers took to Aaron immediately.

I stood on the upper walkway and watched him play below. About twenty feet down the river was a hundred-foot-high bridge. The walkway and that bridge provided two great views for people to stop and watch something they had never seen before.

With hard thrusts on his wheels, he rolled up a ramp about halfway, then made a quick U-turn and went down to pick up speed. Then he went up the other ramp and did the same thing, going back and forth between the two ramps, faster each time. That eventually got him high enough to reach the top of a ramp. He then grabbed that top and pulled himself and his strapped-on chair to the platform. From that height he could drop down and go completely up the opposite ramp. There, he could do a handplant and return to the other ramp or catch the top and pull himself up for another run. He was fast and smooth. It was fun to look down from that walkway and watch him. It was even more fun to see all the spectators stop and stare.

Most of the time, we left Aaron to himself. Having his parents hang around him all the time was not cool. So while we walked the parks, he played on those blue ramps. On one of those days he heard someone yell, "Wheelz!" That was strange to hear in

Wheelz

Germany. It was one of his friends from Woodward. He was shocked to see Aaron down on the Rhine landing tricks.

We were glad to be filming again after the rains stopped. The second day of shooting, he flew up that ramp over the gap onto the arcade table.

He went as fast as he could on that eight-foot table. At the end of the table was a guy holding a giant stuffed panda. He jumped out of the way as Aaron flew off the table.

Aaron's trajectory led him straight to the stairs leading to the huge building. It looked as though he had to crash into those stairs, but he merely lifted three wheels up and made the turn on one wheel, his other wheels floating over the first step.

After the turn, Aaron headed to the stairs that led down to an outdoor cafe. Going down the stairs was the other stunt the stunt crew thought should be handled by one of their own, but they let him do them. He bounced down them with ease on his back wheels then crashed into the cafe tables. When the motorcyclists saw he was surrounded by a crowd, they rode away.

Before we left Düsseldorf, we visited the place where most of the movie was filmed—an old, abandoned factory. Aaron handed out as many Hardcore Sitting shirts and posters as he had. The crew was gracious and sad to see him go. It was especially hard for him to say goodbye to the stunt crew. All in all it was a fun trip.

On our flight home, a flight attendant let me sit in business class with my family. For her kindness, I showed her a video of Aaron and told her he had just finished helping with the movie *Crocodiles of the Suburbs*. She got so excited. She said they had made that film the first time in her hometown—that everyone in Germany loved that story.

She made me show the other flight attendants the video. We landed in Los Angeles one day before the X Games.

The X Games

From early on, doing the X Games was a dream for Aaron. Few venues could get the word out about a new extreme sport like the X Games. We had tried hard to get him into an exhibition for the Dew Games, but with no success. I suggested we set up a booth outside the Dew Games with his videos playing while Aaron held up a piece of cardboard that read, "Will do stunts for games." He didn't appreciate such suggestions.

His opportunity to participate in the X Games came quick. Amy Purdy and Daniel Gale of Adaptive Action Sports set up an adaptive exhibition with the X Games and invited Aaron to participate. When I met Amy, I didn't know she was a double amputee. She walked like everyone else. But when I saw her the next day, she was wearing pants that came down just below her knees, revealing her cool steel legs. It was as though she were showing them off. She seemed to like the look of robotic legs. She could have hidden them, but why? Years later Amy was on *Dancing With The Stars,* displaying her legs and her talents for the world to see.

A few weeks before the games, a PRWeb press release read as follows:

> Aaron Fotheringham & Colours Wheelchairs team up for the X Games
>
> Wheelz

Aaron Fotheringham, 17 years old, is the newest discipline in action sports. . . This is the first time the X Games has featured disabled extreme athletes at their event. There will be 17 disabled athletes: 9 skateboarders and 8 Moto X riders. Fotheringham is the only disabled skateboard athlete that performs his tricks from his wheelchair.

...Fotheringham is the first person to do a backflip in a wheelchair and is planning on doing one at the X Games.... He has been a sponsored athlete with Colours Wheelchairs since the age of 14... Aaron is clearly a pioneer in the wheelchair sports world.... John Box says, "We are hearing people talk about this amazing kid doing tricks in a wheelchair. And people of all ages are imagining what it would be like to do things like Aaron. I don't know the correct word to define Aaron and what he is doing for the disabled. When you watch him people are speechless..... I wonder if Mike Metzger would attempt a backflip in a wheelchair.

When we got there, all Aaron could think about was the MegaRamp. It was forty to fifty feet high. It ended with a ramp that launched a rider over a thirty foot chasm to a landing ramp, then up a vertical wall. I thought he was crazy or just trying to be extreme, but he was serious.

Wheelz

The next best thing was the Big Ramps. They were about twenty-five feet high on two sides with a valley in between. They looked like a giant U. Aaron immediately went to the top of those ramps. To that date, they were the highest ramps he had ever been on. It was a ramp as high as a two story house, but he didn't give it a second thought. They were smooth wood that just looked fun. But for those who had never seen a kid balancing a wheelchair, front wheels up, poised to drop that height, they had lots to think about. He flew down. His speed shot him up the other ramp almost to the top. He then turned down and rolled between the two ramps.

When Shaun White saw him, he said, "That just beat anything I have ever tried!" That was a generous thing to say, and it meant a lot to Aaron coming from one of the greatest skateboarders and snowboarders in the world.

To get into the X Games, they gave us passes to wear around our necks. Aaron got an athlete's pass; mine was an assistant pass. Those passes got us into the food tent, which was the size of a large restaurant. They offered pasta, burgers, hot dogs, fries, chicken, ribs, veggies, fruit, potatoes, beans—you name it—for free. They even had Taco Bell (which Aaron loves) and refrigerators full of drinks. They gave the athletes bags full of energy bars, big headphones, and all sorts of other things. We could watch the Games on a big screen, get on computers, play

Wheelz

arcade games, and eat. Like most of mankind, I love to eat. And a tent full of food was heaven.

With time to kill, I went alone to the X Games huge stadium to watch the motocrossers practice. The stadium seating was virtually empty. The bikers came out one or two at a time and raced the track. When they hit the big dirt jumps, they were a thrill to observe. I sat in a shaded part of the stadium, my arms spread to the seats beside me, on a beautiful California day. I had my own private show.

I love it when they let go of their bikes and float like Superman. Then they catch the back of their seats and pull themselves back onto their bikes just in time to land. It's cool when they turn their bikes on their sides and spin around 180 degrees, then spin back just in time to hit the down ramp. With their flips and spins and no-handers, they were a blast to watch.

A trip to Germany, free admittance to the X Games and a tent full of food was pretty cool. By the time Wheelz was 17 our world was high adventure—especially my wife's because she accompanied him on most of his trips. And yet these things are nothing compared to the numerous posts we have seen like the following.

It is March 30th, 2015; seven years after Aaron filmed that Crocodile movie. Kaylene said, "Listen to this blog from a fan."

Wheelz

Ilaria Naef Ila's Crazy thoughts: How it all started

I was about 15 years old and I spent my days on YouTube watching videos of Ryan Sheckler and skateboarding tutorials. I knew my dream of becoming a skateboarder would never come true: I have Cerebral Palsy. I can barely walk on crutches but I had always wanted to skate. I dragged myself around every day with the help of my crutches or a walker, then I closed my eyes and imagined my life without a disability and with a board under my feet.

Around that time, I got my first wheelchair. I can't walk for a long distance and whenever we had a lot to walk I was pushed around in a baby buggy. I was 15 years old. I didn't like the fact that I couldn't decide where I wanted to go, but walking was so exhausting that I really needed to sit down every once in a while. One day my physical therapist asked me if I would like to get a wheelchair to replace the baby buggy, since I wasn't a baby anymore. I agreed, so she told my family about it. It was not easy for them, because

Wheelz

they saw the wheelchair as something "very disabled" people use, and they didn't see me that way. That is why I didn't use the chair the first year. I did not insist on using the chair more often because I thought walking was tiring but still less limiting.

I was trying to learn German, so I started looking for German movies online and I decided to watch one. One of the main characters was a kid on a wheelchair. I always read the names of the actors after watching a movie. One of those names caught my eye: Aaron Fotheringham, wheelchair stuntman. I wondered what a wheelchair stuntman could do, so I googled his name. The first results were YouTube videos, the titles were something like "Wheelchair in a skateboard park." Needless to say I immediately pressed play. That was the moment that changed the way I see my disability. I couldn't take my eyes off of this kid shredding the park on his chair, with a motocross helmet on his head. At the end of the video, I was so happy I almost cried. It was possible. I could be a skater. Wheelchairs can be cool. IN that moment, I knew I needed to talk to that guy. I found a contact form on his website and sent him an email. I told him how his videos opened the door to a whole

Wheelz

new world for me, a world where dreams do come true. He replied the next day, and seeing his name in my inbox made me the happiest girl on the planet. There was someone telling me it was ok to have a disability, he was telling me there was nothing wrong with me and that the wheelchair was something to play with, it was not a bad thing. I found out he was not the only one hitting the skate park on his chair, there was a whole team, a big family. I started dreaming about becoming a member of that family.

A few weeks later, Aaron told me he would be coming to Italy for a TV show. They were filming in Rome, a 6 hour drive from my town. Not close, but not as far as his hometown, Las Vegas. I begged my parents to take me there. I knew I had to meet that kid. It took me a long time and a lot of effort to persuade them, but they eventually agreed to drive me to Rome.

When I met him, I was blown away by what he could do on his chair. Even my parents were pretty impressed. We talked, played and had fun, and when I left Rome I knew everything was going to be ok, my dreams could come true and I could become the person I had always wanted to be. That was only the beginning: I could be independent and happy. My wheelchair was my favorite thing to play with. My disability was a blessing.

My most recurring thought in that stadium, however, was *I never could have imagined any of this would be our life.* It was a pleasant thought.

On the day of the exhibition, they gave everyone time to practice. There were guys with prosthetic legs on skateboards. There was a guy missing one arm. One guy was blind in one eye. But they all were great at what they did. One young man from Hawaii, Evan Strong, was better than most ablebodied skateboarders I have seen. They were so good it was easy to forget they were disabled. That doesn't necessarily happen with a wheelchair. It was as though this kid in a chair was there with a bunch of great skateboarders. Therefore every trick Aaron did had every eye in the crowd watching him.

In the exhibition, Aaron went hard and fast. He dropped down a fifteen-foot drop, shot across a short bowl, and up the other side. With so much speed, he turned right and rode horizontally for about ten feet at the top of the ramp.

Gravity was pulling him down, forcing him to fall off the wall. I was sure he was going to crash. Wheelz thought so as well. But at the last moment, he turned sharp into the drop and pulled it out. It looked cool. Another trick was his handplant. It was the first time he had done it in a public event, and he landed it squarely. The crowd was astonished.

For his last trick, he sat atop a four-foot-high box above the bowl. He had to clear a two-foot protruding ledge and hit the ramp just beyond it. It was much like the step-down at Pro Park. From the top of the box to the bottom of the bowl was nineteen feet.

I was standing next to the guys who were running the boom camera. They said things like "What is this kid going to do?" "Are you kidding?" "Make sure you get this."

Aaron waited for the skaters to finish their runs. The clock was running down. In the last few seconds of the exhibit, he jumped. I had no question he would land it. He did. But it was rewarding to have a lot of witnesses.

After everyone left, I asked the cameramen if they had gotten the last trick on film. They said they had and it would most likely be on ESPN that evening. We watched for it that night. They covered the MegaRamp and some other events, but they said nothing about the adaptive exhibition. They did show an old interview with Aaron featuring some of his tricks, but nothing on that day.

I thought it ironic. They had obviously been looking for stories to fill time around their various competitions, but they hadn't recognized the story that was right before their eyes. And I'm not just talking about that last trick of Aaron's: the whole exhibition was impressive. All of those skateboarders were good. The X Games were reaching a new community. They were being inclusive. It would have served them well to advertise that. Nevertheless, Aaron had done the X Games, and he had landed everything he'd tried.

A World Record

When I say, "We adopted two children from Moldova," I use the word "we" like a father who says, "We had a baby." In other words, I watched. The mountain of paperwork and red tape required to adopt a child is overwhelming. You have to have a form made from paper responsibly harvested from trees in Oregon, signed by the governor in the presence of the president, witnessed by a White House notary and two F.B.I. agents, and stamped with your state seal. And oh, by the way, you need them in triplicate. Okay, I may be exaggerating a little – but just a little. And that is here in America. In Moldova, my wife had to pay thousands of dollars to get a signature a bureaucrat was supposed to sign as part of her job. The parking attendant charged her 100 dollars to park the car in an empty lot.

That is all a story of its own. But I bring it up because Kaylene did it all in record time. What would have taken six to nine months, she did in three. The adoption agency in America was astounded. Again, when it comes to adopting children, a lion after its prey is a fair analogy for her. Therefore when I mention Aaron's Guinness World Record took her eighteen months to arrange, I am suggesting it was no small feat.

John and Mike Box kept insisting that Aaron get his backflip in the record books. My wife contacted Guinness in September of

Wheelz

2006. She got no response. She tried again in 2007. This time, her email got through. Their first response was in September of 2007. They said they received our proposal and gave her a claim identification number. She then went through the process of registering the claim. In April, 2008 she received the following.

Dear Mrs. Fotheringham,

Thank you for your enquiry regarding your intention to attempt the record for 'wheelchair backflip'. Your proposal is not of interest to us as a new category because we don't monitor 'firsts'. However, we have created the following record which will make the record beatable and therefore acceptable to us: 'Most wheelchair backflips in one minute'.

Guinness World Records

She was instructed to go on their website and get the specific guidelines for setting any record. There were about fifteen pages of rules. Kaylene talked to Joe Wichert about doing the record at an Am Jam competition. The record required a mountain of paperwork, two witnesses, ramp measurements, a timer, still and video cameramen, media coverage, a notary, and more. The easiest part of the event was the flip. Aaron had done it numerous times. But this time was for the record.

On October 25th, 2008, everything came together. The crowd was huge. One of the witnesses was our friend Larry Brown. We all enjoyed witnessing history in the making. Aaron wasn't concerned about hitting the flip; he was nervous about landing it twice in a row. He knew he had time to do two. He wanted to solidly set the record. The idea was once he landed the first one, he needed to hustle up the 200-foot slope and try a second one. He landed the flip three or four times that day but could never do it consecutively.

We were all a little disappointed until Joe Wichert announced, "You need to understand he just set a world record." Aaron tried for two in a row until he was exhausted.

On the way home, Kaylene said she would begin the process for recording the breaking of that record.

On the same day, the BMX Advanced competition was taking place. Aaron had so many Intermediate trophies he didn't care to win any more. But he wanted dearly to win the Advanced.

The kids in that group were pro. Because the riding conditions are perfect in Vegas, the riders are good. To even be allowed to compete in BMX Advanced was a big deal.

In an interview about six months before the competition, Joe Weichert said to Ken Ritter, an Associated Press writer, "People don't just say, 'He's in a wheelchair; put him on the podium.' He's had to work his way up. Definitely no one's giving him a free ride – absolutely not. The kid earns it."

Despite being worn out by his attempts to set that record Aaron had a good day. With his backflip, fifteen-foot drop in, and handplant, he won.

On the way home, he was disappointed he hadn't gotten two flips in a row for the record.

I said, "I don't know – a world record and first place in Advanced BMX is not a bad day."

He said, "I guess I need to look at it that way."

Dear Manu,

By the way, he also took first place in BMX Advanced at the competition that day. That means he can no longer participate in Am Jam competitons Sad, but he will survive. I will simply need to work harder to find other opportunities for him to "show off." Let me know if you hear of anything.

Kaylene

Wheelz

When the record came out, on his certificate and in the book, it read, "Aaron Fotheringham landed the first wheelchair backflip." I guess now and then the Guinness people do have firsts. Thank heavens he hadn't landed two. It would have read, "Two-in-a-minute record." Since that day I have seen or heard of a number of successful wheelchair backflips. But he will always and forever hold the official world's record for being the first.

Leeder O. Men

I was sitting in my office when Vanessa Huff stopped in for a visit. She was a student of mine when I first started teaching in Las Vegas. Now she is a lawyer and a mother. When she came to visit, she brought her thirteen-year-old son John with her.

He stood for a moment, fidgeting with his hands. Then his eyes opened wide and he said, "Are you really Wheelz's dad?"

I couldn't help but smile inside. "Yes, I am!" I walked over to my filing cabinet, pulled out the *Sports Illustrated* issue, and turned to his page.

John said, "I went to the skate park the other day and all the kids said I had just missed him. I was kind of bummed."

"I'm sorry you missed him. If I hear what park he's going to, would you like me to let you know?"

"Yeah, that would be rad. I mean, if it's okay with you."

Vanessa rubbed John's shoulder. "Call me, and wherever he goes I'll get my son there. He's a huge fan."

Wheelz

This BMXer's hero is on a wheelchair. Who would have ever guessed? The answer to that question is John Lytle, the creator of *Leeder O. Men.*

John was born in Elgin, Illinois, in 1964. Every summer his mom would take him and his two brothers and two sisters to northern Wisconsin. While they were on one trip in particular, she made an offer on a little resort. The offer was accepted and her family ended up running a resort surrounded by dense pines and beautiful lakes.

John's cousin visited their resort every year from Chicago. In 1976 when she came to visit, she brought a skateboard. It was the first skateboard that John had ever seen. Once she let John try it, she couldn't pry it from him. So she went into KMart, took a skateboard off the rack, didn't pay for it, rode it out of the store, and said "Here you go." When she left, John was probably the only kid in Wisconsin that rode a skateboard at that time.

He got skateboarding magazines from the school library and studied the ramps. In one of the magazines, he found a photo of a halfpipe and showed it to his brother. After one look, John's brother said, "I think I can build one of those."

When that halfpipe was finished they couldn't get John off of the thing. John's mom would sit with his dog and watch him practice for hours. When John was fourteen, his family started spending

Wheelz

their winters in California. He attended school, but the majority of his time was spent on his skateboard.

One winter John's mom stayed in Wisconsin to sell the resort. When John's sister didn't hear from her for a couple days, she went to see why. She found her at the resort with an empty bottle of aspirin and an excruciating headache. It took a while for the doctors to figure everything out, but when they did, the family learned that she had brain cancer. John was hurled back home, into a dreadful situation.

Eight months later, John was nineteen and basically on his own. His mother had lost her battle with cancer. Ready to face the world head on, John traveled the United States in a 1974 Chevy Vega that by some miracle kept going. He entered skateboard contests on backyard ramps from 1982 to 1985. It didn't take long before he started placing and became well-known among skateboarders.

Well-known was great, but John's dream was to go professional. He practiced day and night for years until he realized he was getting older and not progressing as much as he hoped.

Even though he knew his dreams of going pro were a long shot, John didn't want to leave the skateboard world behind, so he started making little magazines. The industry called them "zines."

Zines are small, self-published articles with text and images. He pumped them out on a photocopier.

For several years he published a zine called *Naughty Nomad.* Everywhere he went he took pictures, wrote articles, and published his little magazines. He sent his zines to the friends he had met in his travels. He loved doing it because the zines were about skateboarding with creativity.

John also sent his articles to *Thrasher Magazine* in San Francisco. They had a section called "The Zine Thing." It turned out he wasn't the only one doing it. The magazine had about twenty-five different zines. John was amazed by the underground network of zines.

That was when he enrolled in Santa Barbara City College in California. One semester he needed a credit to fill his class schedule and the only class that fit was at an adaptive weight training class. He had no idea what adaptive weight training meant, but he showed up to the class and was surprised to see a bunch of disabled individuals working out on weightlifting gear.

The instructor looked at him strangely. "What are you doing here?"

He said, "Well, I need this credit. This class works for me. Can I join?"

Wheelz

The instructor smiled, "That's fine with me. I can use you as an assistant." That was the first day of the rest of John Lytle's new life.

It didn't take long for John to start making friends in the class. He met and got close to a bunch of people with significant challenges, challenges that John had never thought about. As the assistant, John would spot them on the bench press. He lifted them up, still attached to their chairs, to do pull-ups. Instead of feeling sorry for themselves, these people were living life, but they didn't take themselves too seriously. They were always joking around. It added another layer to his thinking about what adversity really is and what life is about. The only one in the class that felt sorry for himself was John, when it ended.

While John loved his adaptive training class, he spent most of his time in another class doodling on drawings for his magazines. One day he drew a caricature of one of the guys from his adaptive class sitting in a wheelchair. He put that picture into a drawing of an empty pool. Then he drew his character doing the equivalent of a skateboard aerial (wich is similar to a handplant), and the lights came on. As John stared at the upside-down wheelchair hovering over the slick, dry pool, he thought, *Oh my word, is this possible? Could a person in a wheelchair accomplish the same thing that I did on my skateboard?*

That was when the obsession set in. John started drawing wheelchairs in all kinds of skateboard situations. He called his main character Leeder O. Men. Leeder belonged to a cartoon family where everyone was a skateboarder, even the mother. But Leeder was in a wheelchair. His mission was to figure out how to skate in a wheelchair to go with the flow with his family. They had a house full of ramps. Everything in the house was skateable. The fireplace had transitions. Leeder's whole life was about transitions.

John put the Leeder comics in his magazines and they resonated with people. He started getting a cult following. John was proud of the concept and showed off his watercolor paintings to anyone who seemed interested.

The following was great and John loved having fans, but he needed a job. He wrote to *Thrasher Magazine*. When they learned he was the author of *Naughty Nomad*, they offered him a job.

After three years, John quit *Thrasher* and toured with a band in Europe as their guitarist. After the music tour, he came back to America and started a new tour, writing a book on dilapidated ranches and homes in ghost towns. It fascinated him that these little towns, out in nowhere, had once thrived.

At thirty-five, John married Claire, a beautiful girl from France. He settled down with her and started doing freelance graphics and web design.

Wheelz

One day while rummaging through some old stuff, Claire found John's *Leeder O. Men* drawings. She was working at a hospital with disabled people at the time. It was kind of an epiphany for her when she considered who she was working with and how relevant these drawings would be to some of them.

She had a lot of questions. John was happy to talk about it and the conversation reinvigorated him. He was so focused on supporting his family and paying the bills that he had not thought about Leeder for a long time. A lot of emotions came up when Claire pulled those drawings out, and John had to do something about them. He figured he'd put his drawings online and see what might happen with them. He came up with the domain name Dizabled. That was in 1995. People responded in a way he never imagined. He started to put the word out to different disability magazines.

John decided to draw real cartoons in earnest. He bought a book on cartooning. He began looking at comics in the paper more closely. He immersed himself in disability websites and disability news to get himself up-to-date with all the pressing issues. John knew he had to draw those cartoons, but he also knew the world wasn't ready for them and not everyone was going to love his work. He had to be careful. He didn't want to offend anybody. A handful of people didn't appreciate that he was trying to place himself in their position when he had no disability.

Wheelz

That was when John found an ally named Patty Wooten. She worked at a place called the Association for Applied and Therapeutic Humor. Her organization basically supported him in his efforts to do Leeder without getting harassed. They didn't actually defend him in any practical sense, but he just deferred any naysayers to that association so he didn't have to deal with them.

Of course, it would still hurt when someone sent a negative email It didn't happen a lot, but when it did he was like, "Oh my word, another one."

John needed a way to get rid of those nasty emails, so he made a place on his website called the Leeder O. Phobes. It was a black dungeon. It had a porthole in the top and Leeder looking into it, with the blue sky behind him. That's the world where dark comments would go. That page is still online.

John penned about 200 cartoons and submitted them to all the syndicates. They were starting to look like real cartoon strips and people were catching on. That was from 1996 to 1998. Aaron was five in 1996.

The syndicates told him, "Hundreds are not enough. If you want to be in the paper you've got to produce thousands. We need to know you can do this for a long time."

So John went to work on his Leeder series with everything he had. A lot of people were coming to his website, so he promised a new cartoon every week.

Then in 1998 it all came to an abrupt end when John got a call from his brother that his sister had been murdered. She worked as a T.V. news reporter for a station in Temple, Texas. It turns out that she had a stalker in her apartment complex. One day, the stalker broke in and found her in the shower. He stabbed her sixteen times. Thankfully, he was caught and imprisoned for life.

But John's life turned into a prison of its own. His creativity died with his sister. He had a wife and a son to support. He no longer thought he could dedicate the amount of time, effort, and emotional energy that Leeder needed.

People wondered what had happened. He tried to explain the situation to them on his website. He didn't want to have people coming back to the site and finding that there was nothing new. But that's what ended up happening.

Instead of shutting the website down, John decided to just leave Leeder online. What he didn't expect is that Leeder would continue to live a life of his own. People would still find him and learn from him. To them, it was all new and there was still enough material for them to enjoy the site.

Wheelz

Periodically, John got emails requesting permission to reprint the cartoons, and soon, Leeder was showing up in countless newsletters. John collected files full of the newsletters and magazines that printed the cartoon.

People would call him and say, "I'm a physical therapist. Can I use your cartoons for a presentation?"

John would always say, "Of course," and never charge anything. There were some who accused him of being in it for the money because he offered a ten-dollar t-shirt on his site. Those people ended up in the dungeon. Even as John died inside, Leeder and his optimistic outlook lived on.

Years later John told me, "I always believed that someone would one day come along and not feel like a wheelchair was a wheelchair, but more like a set of wheels. When Aaron came up on the radar, I watched a YouTube video of him and cried. I cried like a baby. It was such a profound moment to realize my vision wasn't just an abstract idea, that it was human. In a strange way I didn't feel alone anymore."

John contacted us for the first time in May of 2007.

    Dear Kaylene and Aaron,

I am so happy to finally get in contact with you both. With a warm heart, I have been following the progression of Aaron and I express my support for the personal philosophy that emanates from the Fotheringhams. Aaron, you are truly one unique individual. I have waited 20 years for the fictional artwork to become reality. I always knew this day would come.

John wanted to interview Aaron and take photos of him for his Leeder website. So he came and stayed with us a few days. He knew what Aaron could do at skate parks, but what thrilled him was that Aaron had the same indomitable spirit and humor that he remembered from his friends in his adaptive weight training class. It was the same spirit that Leeder had.

John now makes websites for some high-profile companies. He built and still maintains Aaron's website. If I want to learn about what Wheelz is doing, I go there.

That someone would imagine someone on a wheelchair at a skate park is not that incredible. But to think such a kid would change the world--to assume that playing around at a skate park would make him a leader-blows me away. Even when I knew Aaron was exceptional and saw him as a role model, I was still blinded. I couldn't see him in any significant role of influence.

Wheelz

Aaron resented my saying he was a role model because that was not why he practiced at skate parks. I think he instinctively knew if that was his goal he would not succeed. He was there to play and improve. But I also think deep inside he always knew who he was.

There's a small treasure chest in the corner of our bedroom. It is packed with news articles and other memorabilia about our son. Somewhere deep in that chest is a journal entry of a five-year-old about walking on his hands. He exhorted others to try it. He gave cautions. He was writing to followers.

"Gimps rule" wasn't a defense. It was an invitation to share a vision. When he started publishing videos they always began with horrendous crashes. He didn't want anyone to follow without understanding the costs. He always acted like a leader, but never liked it when I brought it up.

John wasn't the only one to put two and two together. The following is part of an article by Skate and Annoy.

> One of the stories being recycled on CNN (TV) today is footage of some guys at the Winter X Games doing backflips on snowmobiles. Whatever. Get back to me when you do it in a pickup truck. In the meantime, in a case of life catching up to skateboarding, a 14-year-old kid named Aaron Fotheringham has completed a backflip on
>
> Wheelz

his wheelchair. What do I mean by life catching up to skateboarding? I'm talking about the character known as *Leeder O. Men* from the '80s skate zine known as *Naughty Nomads*. Although fictional, Leeder was the first guy to ride vert on a wheelchair. There have been admirable, but mostly tame videos on the web of guys in wheelchairs at skate parks. Aaron seems to be taking it to another level.

Aaron calls his activities Hardcore Sitting, or Wheelchair Skateboarding, but curiously he says he draws more influence from BMX. He seems to have a good sense of humor too.

ND: Was the first jump without cushions successful?

Aaron: Almost, but my momentum threw me on my back. It took me about 15 more times before I landed it squarely. But it doesn't matter because I still can't walk.

Just kidding, I'm doing fine.

Aaron seems like he's got his head on straight. . . . Hopefully Aaron will buck the trend of the Extreme Jock attitude. He's already ducking out of one popularity contest, as he won't ride without a helmet. Apparently he's seen too many broken teeth and gouged skulls.

Leeder is the creation of John Lytle. . .John has taken some heat for daring to make a comic about a disabled character while being able-bodied himself.

> "Your comics stink, I hate them. You think we are just product placement or some sick, twisted way to make money off of the misery me and so many others go through. You should be ashamed of yourself. So should everyone else who likes your comics. I hope you have to live in a wheelchair. Try spending your life in this sick, twisted little chair."

In his defense, well, he doesn't really need any.

He's got more admirers than detractors. The first time I saw Leeder, it made perfect sense to me. Leeder was a person who refused to be restrained by the rigid roles defined by our society. .

.

The similarities between John's cartoon character and Aaron are uncanny. There are dozens but I will mention only one. Years ago when I saw Aaron's green florescent chair, my initial thought was *That's an obnoxious color.* But it made sense. Society said, "Don't stare at kids in wheelchairs." He said, "Hey, over here."

Aaron never saw that Leeder cartoon until I pointed it out to him years after he'd been riding his signature green chair. The fact that

Wheelz

Leeder's chair was the exact shade and color of green is a little creepy!

My kid being a cartoon character that came to life is a lot weird and a little cool. That he is a leader in his own way is very cool.

In Psalms it says we can "be like a tree planted by the rivers of water, that bringeth forth his fruit in his season" (Psalms 1:3). Surely this is a promise of influence, because the fruit of a tree is for everyone but the tree. For years I did not see my son as a giving tree and I definitely never considered any rivers. A tree is nothing without water. I love that Aaron can help change someone's outlook on life, but he could never have done it alone. There have been so many rivers that have nourished and moved him along. I don't believe John foresaw that. Nor do I think John envisioned he would be one of them.

Aaron travels the world and is sustained by multiple rivers. I could give a hundred examples. Here is one. In August of 2009 John Box requested that Aaron perform at a convention called the Abilities Expo in Anaheim, California. Colours paid about 20,000 dollars to have ramps made. A professional ramp builder built them for about half price. They were huge and spanned about a hundred feet. Joe Wickert and Kaylene corresponded with the builder numerous times, working out their design. Wheelz was on a chair that Mike Box continually improved for him. He had wheels from DT Swiss, tires from Schawlbe, front suspension from Frog Legs and Fox Shocks. He wore helmets and pads from Six Six One and other sponsors who he never dared approach on his own behalf. In other words, people like Joe Wickert, Sam Abraham, and Mike Box got him his sponsors.

While he performed in that Anaheim show, *Last Call with Carson Daly* came and did a piece on him. Other news stations came and interviewed him as well. Ellen Stohl, who has the distinction of being the first and only disabled girl to show up in *Playboy*, described what she saw for readers of *Disabled Dealer Magazine*:

> Every time I hear about Aaron or see a video of him, I get goose bumps. I mean, here is a kid who has used a wheelchair for mobility since he was 3; carving, grinding, power-sliding and doing 180s like nobody's business. He sits at the top of the skateboard/bike ramp, pushes off, rips down one side then up the other, where he handplants a perfect 180. The chair strapped to his legs flies up off the ramp and into the air as Aaron supports the whole movement with one hand. Then zip, zap, the wheels are back on the ground and Aaron glides to the other section of the ramp, where he stops and prepares for his next trick. And what a trick it is. With the strength of his arms, limited movement in his legs and support from his father [I handed him his chair after he got up the ramp], Aaron climbs the ladder to the high end of the ramp, straps himself into the chair and then pushes off;

Wheelz

down he goes, gaining speed as he traverses the steep incline. Then it's up the other side and into the air where he completes a 360-degree backflip before his wheels find their way back to earth. It's an incredible sight and everyone who sees it realizes that the limits to how far we can go are much farther than we ever imagined! [v]

Wheelz did that routine every hour. In between runs he signed autographs and talked to the press. He did his part. When the show was over, Aaron wanted the ramps. So Moe sent a semi truck and the ramps filled the trailer. Moe charged us for gas and his driver's time (which was nothing) and then stored the ramps for free in one of his warehouses.

The expo drew its largest crowd ever. An article about Wheelz at the expo showed up in the *Wall Street Journal*.[vi].

The barrier around the ramp was surrounded by kids on wheelchairs, every one of them looking up to my boy. One of them was a four-year-old named Hunter Pochop. I met him and his mother at a skate park five years later. When I did, I asked her about her son.

She said, "My eldest son saw Aaron at a church conference called Especially for Youth in Las Vegas. He called and said, 'Mom, you need to check him out.' So we went to see him at the Abilities Expo in Anaheim. Last year Hunter did a report for his third-

Wheelz

grade class about his hero, who was of course Aaron. The class was then assigned to write a bio about their heroes. The teacher wouldn't let him use Wheelz because there is no book written about him. So he wrote about Tony Hawk."

Aaron would take it as a compliment to know Tony Hawk was Hunter's second choice. Anyway, Hunter's life was changed for the better because of that Anaheim event. I am sure there were others. The *Wall Street Journal* has a pretty good readership. My simple point is that Aaron did not do these things on his own. And no one could have predicted the kind of influence that would come from a kid playing on a wheelchair at a skate park. Well, actually, someone did predict it.

The Speech

"Thanks for being an inspiration, Aaron. All my excuses have been rendered invalid!" EnticeMedia (After video blog)

Like I said before, if someone ends up doing a handplant I'll be impressed. So when we saw John's cartoon character doing a handplant, Kaylene and I equated Leeder with Aaron. But even after we met John, even after we made those connections, the leader part had still not dawned on us. To us Aaron was just playing around and was good at what he did. But little by little, year after year, we became more and more convinced he was the one that would indeed personify that cartoon. We got a glimpse when he gave his first speech.

On July 3rd, 2007, Bruce Davey, codirector of the 2008 National Adapted Physical Education Conference, contacted us through John Lytle. John was already speaking at their conference and suggested they include Aaron. Bruce asked Aaron to speak in San Diego a year and a half in advance. That gave Aaron plenty of time to get ready for another challenge—public speaking.

P.E. teachers are some of the nicest people in the world. They are definitely a great group to speak to. They are upbeat, love life, and want to help children. It was a great audience for Aaron's first major address.

When Bruce Davey contacted Aaron, Aaron didn't want to do it. But he figured he would have enough time to prepare, and if he wanted to promote his sport, he'd have to do it eventually. As the time drew closer, he was more nervous. He did not feel any more prepared than when he originally accepted the request to speak, but he was on the program. He couldn't back out.

He started his speech by saying, "I was born November 8th, 1991. I tell you this so you won't forget my birthday again next year." Everyone always wants to know how he got into the sport, so he began by talking about his brother. He then described how he had progressed from trick to trick.

Part way through, he showed a two-minute video of the early years. He talked a little more and then showed his Verses video, which features his first backflips. Halfway through, the projector stopped. While they worked on fixing it, he said, "I guess I ought to do something." He got out of his chair and stood on his hands. He then did push-ups with his legs still in the air. For the 300 or more P.E. teachers, it was a hit.

While the second video was playing, I had two thoughts: 1) For those who weren't aware of what he did, these videos let them know their speaker was an expert in his field; 2) People wanted to know about Aaron's mom. That was obvious because so many people kept looking over at her. My thoughts were verified when they asked her to speak. They asked about her fears. She said she

Wheelz

was in no different position from any other mother who had a child at a skate park, but she did express gratitude because he always wore a helmet.

Between the humor, improvisation, the videos, and the mom, it was an inspiring speech and a great conclusion for an Adapted Physical Education Conference.

A teacher came up to me afterwards and told me about a boy whose disability level was equal to Aaron's. "He is so discouraged. All he does is play video games." But after seeing Aaron speak, the teacher told me he planned to talk to the boy about all of his possibilities.

Aaron ended his speech with this: "Many people see a wheelchair as confining. I see it as an extreme sport." It was a message he would repeat whenever anyone let him speak.

Aaron generally resents me trying to give him advice with his sport. But because I'm a teacher, Aaron listens to me in this area. Before each speech he goes over it with me. I have taught him to take his time and explain the details as much as he remembers of each story—to enjoy the attention in front of a crowd. That day in San Diego went well. Since then he has steadily improved.

Years later he spoke to a group of about 250 teenagers. He had fun with that speech. His humor flowed easily and naturally. He

Wheelz

said, after describing a terrible crash, "I was so angry I wanted to throw my chair. But I figured I'd just have to crawl over to get it, so I didn't."

After his speeches I would usually give him a few pointers. For that speech I had nothing to offer. After Aaron's San Diego speech the following was left on John's website by Joel Anderson.

Just came back from our 37th National Adapted Physical Education Conference in San Diego, CA, where both John Lytle and Aaron Fotheringham were keynote speakers. I would just like to say to both of you... keep shredding up the pavement and the paper... you guys ROCK and are a major inspiration to so many people with and without disabilities.

Joel C. Anderson

Adapted Physical Education Specialist

Joel added this quote from Theodore Roosevelt: "Far better is it to dare mighty things, to win glorious triumphs, even though checkered with failure, than to rank with those poor spirits who neither enjoy much nor suffer much, because they live in the gray twilight
that knows no victory or defeat."

I included this note because of the cool quote from President Roosevelt. He reminds me of a distant cousin of his, Franklin D.

Wheelz

Roosevelt, who was the only United States president who used a wheelchair. In public, the White House made it clear that any images of FDR should not include the wheelchair, and he generally refused to be photographed in his chair. Apparently I wasn't the only one who couldn't envision a leader in a wheelchair.

Unbreakable Chair

For setting a world record and bringing favorable recognition to Las Vegas, the mayor and city council gave Aaron the key to the city. In truth it was Aaron who was getting all the recognition.

For example, one day Kaylene was contacted by twelve different news agencies. These included *CBS This Morning*, CNN, *People*, Germany's RTL Television, and England's BBC Radio.

Two-thousand-eight ended with *CBS This Morning* coming to Las Vegas to shoot footage of Aaron and John Box announcing Woodward West was considering a Hardcore Sitting week for sometime in 2010.

John Box sold Colours Wheelchairs in March of 2008. They kept him on for a year then he resigned.

After John sold his company Colours kept Mike Box on for six months to teach them what he knew and then let him go. He found himself in his fifth marriage, with little in the bank and no job. To his credit, he didn't return to alcohol.

He didn't know what to do with his life, so life kind of dictated his course. Many past customers came to him for repairs. He had built a relationship with so many of them. When they had needs they came to him. And no one needed Mike more than Aaron. He was still torturing chairs. They were much improved but they still needed Mike's help.

Years before the Colours sale I was sitting in their showroom when Mike said, "Now that Aaron is so well-known, we are prepared to pay him to be his sponsor."

I said, "There is no way we will ever do that. You supported him when he was a nobody. As far as we are concerned we will always be in your debt."

Mike increased our debt when, at this low time in his life, he still took care of our boy. To be honest I didn't have a clue he was jobless. We thought Mike was fine. He wasn't fine, but he supported Aaron regardless. His wife Alison finally convinced him that since he was repairing chairs all the time, he ought to start his own company, so he started Box Wheelchairs.

It took him a while to get off the ground, but Mike knows wheelchairs, so it did. All the while Aaron kept breaking his chairs and Mike kept improving them. Without an unbreakable chair no one could participate in the sport Aaron invisioned. It was also crucial because the next chapter in Aaron's life would take him to heights that would require a chair that doesn't break. From those heights, Wheelz became the most famous wheelchair athlete in the world. That wouldn't hurt Mike's business at all.

Wheelz

Nitro Circus

When John Lytle met Aaron they talked for hours. What thrilled John was that Aaron had the psychological traits he had envisioned in Leeder. Wheelz had goals that were huge. He had his sights on the largest ramp in the world--the MegaRamp. That was the center of their conversations. They were both thrilled at the possibilities.

There was a large ramp at an action trade show in San Diego. John convinced Aaron to come to the show. "I think you're going to be in this world someday and I need to make some introductions. Come check out this ramp."

Aaron flew to San Diego. When Wheelz saw the mini MegaRamp, he just stared at it for the longest time.

There was a huge halfpipe set up at the trade show. Wheelz pulled his chair to the top of that ramp. No one knew what to make of a kid on a wheelchair at the top of a large ramp. No one realized he wanted to drop in, so no skateboarder or BMXer gave him a turn, and he was too polite to barge in. He sat there while they all did their runs.

Finally John stood at the base of the ramp and yelled, "Hey, we're trying to do something here."

Wheelz

There was an announcer at the show, so when Aaron dropped in, he got excited and announced what was going on. When Wheelz shot up the other side of the pipe and did his handplant, the announcer went crazy. He had no time to react; he just blurted out his astonishment and sent the place into an uproar. That was Aaron's debut into the action sports world.

John continued to try to get Wheelz a chance on a MegaRamp. He called Bob Burnquist and Danny Way and they both couldn't see it. But Travis Pastrana could. Travis had been in a wheelchair for a year after busting his ankle. That may have helped Aaron's cause. When he saw Aaron on YouTube, he thought, *Heck, yeah. This guy could definitely do a huge ramp*--in particular *Nitro Circus*'s Giganta Ramp.

Kaylene and I were asleep. Aaron was reading comments on his website when all of a sudden he freaked out. He woke us up with, "*Nitro Circus*, do you guys know what this is?" We had no clue.

Nitro Circus is a show on MTV. It's a bunch of highly skilled, slightly crazy stuntmen on motorcycles, BMX bikes, and skateboards who do amazing tricks. The bikers and skateboarders go down a fifty-foot ramp to get the speed they need to do their tricks. The star of *Nitro Circus* is Travis Pastrana--to Aaron and many fans, the god of extreme sports.

Dov Ribnick, the producer for *Nitro*, was asking Aaron if he would like to try their Giganta Ramp (*Nitro*'s name for the MegaRamp).

There is a phone call I'm sure millions of young athletes have dreamt of. It is a coach on the other end of the line inviting him or her to be on a professional team. I was young enough and naive enough to have that dream only to eventually collide with reality--I am more suited to be a jockey than a baseball player. Nevertheless, it was a sweet dream--to be on the field, under the lights, getting paid to play--I know so many people can relate to.

Well, my son got that call. And none of us could sleep. A few days later Dov wrote to Kaylene.

> Hi Kaylene,
>
> My name is Dov Ribnick, I work on the show *Nitro Circus*. As I'm sure Aaron has told you, we are interested in bringing him out to hit a ramp we built outside San Diego. I'm sure you have questions about how big it is, where, what, who, etc. Please feel free to call to discuss. He mentioned he is going to be in San Diego on December 13, and I would like to look into keeping him here for an extra day or two to see how he goes on the ramp and hang with the cast. So I guess just give me a shout and I can

figure out how to keep him here and answer any other questions. Thanks so much, Kaylene!

Dov Ribnick (12/09/09)

The invitation was real. In a documentary narrated by Ed Asner called *Courage in Sports*, they described Aaron's induction into *Nitro Circus*:

VIDEO 5: Is the documentary called *Courage in Sports*.

http://goo.gl/QLTFCv

The documentary begins by quoting Travis Pastrana: "This guy in a wheelchair says he can go down the MegaRamp. The first time I saw Wheelz at a skate park, I thought, *Oh, this guy can definitely do it.*

John Lytle drove to San Diego to support Aaron and film the attempt. They stayed in the same hotel as the *Nitro* team. At breakfast they talked to the team a little. When they heard he was attempting the ramp, they didn't know what to think. They expressed some doubts. John assured them if anyone could do it Aaron could.

Wheelz

When Aaron arrived at the ramp, he had to stick his head out of the car window to see the top of it. It looked huge in real life.

At the bottom of the ramp is a forty-foot gap. You have to make that gap to a landing ramp or foam pit to survive. If you don't clear the gap you can get seriously hurt. Riders crash in the gap all the time.

Dusty Wygle of *Nitro Circus* put it simply: "[It's] a little nerve-wracking."

Travis had suggested they give this kid a chance. Dov had agreed, but when Aaron got there Dov had second thoughts. If Aaron got hurt everyone would question what he was thinking, not to mention the liability. He suggested they lower Aaron halfway down the ramp with a rope and let him go just up to the gap, and then pull him to a stop. Aaron would have nothing to do with that. It seemed riskier than the regular jump. Aaron and John had to do a lot of convincing to get them to let him try.

Commenting on Aaron's first attempt down the ramp, Travis said, "The amazing part about Wheelz – I've never seen so many, you know, gnarly people so scared out of their mind like, 'Don't let him do it. No, we can't do this.' We just didn't know. No one's ever done that."

Aaron told me it looked a lot scarier from the top. A lot of the guys were trying to prepare him and give him advice.

He thought, *I'd better just go before I talk myself out of this.*

He had dreamt for so long about this. He wasn't about to let his fears get in his way. He knew he couldn't afford to think about it. So before they thought he was ready, while they were still offering him advice, he pushed forward and dropped in.

On the way down Aaron realized he had so much speed he needed to do something cool, so at his highest point in the middle of the gap, he did what looked like a slow motion backflip. It was beautiful. He landed squarely on his wheels in the foam pit and everyone yelled.

They caught it all on film. Aaron, to the camera, exclaimed, "That was the coolest thing ever."

One crew member said, "He just did a backflip in a wheelchair—first time down."

Everyone ran up and gave him high-fives and said, "That's the fastest anyone's ever made it into *Nitro Circus*—with one jump." John Lytle was so excited he ran around the ramp four times.

Wheelz

Ed Asner on the same program said, "Courage can be defined in a multitude of ways. Risking life and limb isn't necessarily one of them. But blazing a trail where no one else has ever gone before certainly is."

Travis was quoted saying, "Wheelz is pioneering a whole new sport – a whole new mentality."

Travis's cousin, Greg Powell, who according to Aaron can do anything, said, "A lot of people act towards a guy who is wheelchair-bound as if that is supposed to be an issue and a problem. Wheelz is saying exactly the opposite."

Travis concluded, "He's been able to accomplish what no one even fathomed. They didn't think it was possible. There is no precedence. There's no one on the tour that gets a bigger ovation or that is respected more than Aaron 'Wheelz' Fotheringham. And that's pretty cool. "

Three days before Christmas in 2009, *Nitro Circus* officially invited Aaron to go on their Australian tour. On the same day, Kaylene started lining up Frog Legs for the tour. She also began setting up visas and insurance for Australia. All of this was on top of designing ramps for Italy Guinness World Records.

On the same day, Troy Lee Designs expressed interest again in being Wheelz's helmet sponsor. Their timing was perfect. He would need them a lot. Aaron went to see Mike Box to start building two new chairs for the 2010 spring tour.

On Christmas Day, *Nitro* offered a contract to Aaron. Kaylene had no doubt that she was in over her head. She had to find an agent. The New Year began with Spinergy offering to sponsor Aaron. Saying goodbye to DT Swiss was difficult for Kaylene. Their wheels and their support were great. She told them if they ever made the entire wheelchair wheel she would love to use them. Aaron had a good-sized team behind him. All he had to do was land that flip on the real ramp.

> From Dov (Feb/15/2010)
>
> Also, I have some great news for you guys. We are going in the total opposite direction than keeping Aaron's jumps quiet. We are promoting the heck out of it..We are putting together a commercial of all the highlights, with Anthony, Travis, Jake, and Aaron, so please feel free to tell anyone of your sponsors, tell any engagements you speak to, and any orgs in OZ that you are with us. Our PR manager will be in touch, I am sure, as we want to get it out there, so we are all pumped on that!

Kaylene thought it would be a shame for Aaron to be in all those cities and not visit any children. She asked Dov if she could offer Aaron's services to local spina bifida clinics. Dov loved the idea and Aaron was willing. She contacted a group in each city, but

Wheelz

they didn't know anything about Wheelz, so she sent them video links. Before long each city wanted him to visit their kids. The Australian tour was *Nitro*'s first tour. It would include a kid called Wheelz.

The Coach

Since that Christmas day Wheelz has traveled the world many times over with *Nitro Circus*. If he wanted a vehicle to promote his sport he found one. Before *Nitro* does a tour they send out a P.R. team for publicity. Because Aaron is so unique he is always part of those teams. There's always a news station in every city that wants to interview him.

Aaron was asked to speak in Washington State at a spina bifida fundraiser. Megan Puddy gave an introduction for Aaron. I didn't know he participated in that fundraiser. I was unaware of all the activities Aaron was involved in that Megan lists. It became impossible to keep up. What follows is a small segment of that introduction.

March/20/2010

These days, Aaron travels everywhere. He's due in Australia next month, and I really think every time I hear from him, he's off to some exotic crazy location. But the crazy thing is, he isn't traveling for himself. He travels wherever he can make a difference. He's done a lot of fundraisers, like this one. He does each and every one because he cares. He recently participated in Red Bluff, a fundraiser for disabled sports programs. He does a lot of Hardcore Sitting demos for disabled groups. These are the things that we think of when we think of the difference

Wheelz

that Aaron makes, the difference that he makes to those in the disabled community and those in wheelchairs, but he's done so much more.

Even while Aaron has the whole world calling for him to do demos and to show off his incredible skills, he still finds time to be a counselor and a mentor at various camps. He recently did just that at the Bay Area Junior Wheelchair Camp, and he's also involved in the JAWS camp. He makes time for people like my brother, who don't necessarily care about the backflip but who are thrilled when he will sit down and work on a wheelchair with him. Yesterday, Aaron and Zac went shopping for wheelchair helmets. While some people might consider being in a wheelchair to negatively impact a person's life, Aaron shows Zac how much fun it is to shop for a helmet, or to alter the wheelchair so that it absorbs the shock better when my brother wheels off some cliff following Aaron. One of Aaron's passions is showing children how a wheelchair can be a toy, not just a restriction. And that's meant far more in my life, and in my brother's life, than any of the mind-blowing tricks that Aaron has accomplished.

During that same ESPN segment where I first met Aaron, Aaron was asked how he defines spina bifida. Aaron replied, "An amazing opportunity." That's the person that

I'm proud to have here with me today. His actions inspire the world by showing all of us just how much you can do if you choose to act on what you can do instead of being limited by what you can't. My brother hated stairs because a wheelchair can't go down stairs. But Aaron can simply fly over them, and in watching Aaron, my brother regained that part of the world.

I was sitting in a gym watching Joey (Aaron's younger brother) in some adaptive sports event when in rolled this kid on the back two wheels of his wheelchair. He just flew in, enjoying the smooth floor, like he owned the place.

I said to my wife, "He looks like Aaron."

She said, "He's Blake. Aaron met him before. He actually coached him once at Pro Park."

If there was anyone who could do what Aaron did, it could have been this kid, Blake.

Looking through Aaron's papers, I found an article about the two of them in a local magazine called *Desert Saints*. The article began like this:

"Drop in here, a little higher, higher, right here by this crack." This was the expert instruction given to 8-year-old Wheelz

Blake Dickensen as he edged his wheelchair to the point of no return at the bowl of a Las Vegas skate park for the first time, on a 106-degree August day. As much of an adrenaline rush as it was for Blake to "drop in" at the skate park, it was even more exciting to him that his expert instructor for the day was none other than *Nitro Circus* star and fellow Hardcore Sitter, Aaron Fotheringham.[vii]

There are two pictures with the article. The first is Aaron meeting Blake. In the picture Blake's chair has those safety wheels on. In the second picture those wheels are off as Aaron and Blake roll towards the ramps. Whenever Aaron coached anyone, the first thing that had to go, often to the consternation of cautious mothers, was those wheels.

Perhaps the most repeated question we, as Aaron's parents, have been asked is "Weren't you afraid of him being hurt?" I assume parents of football players are seldom asked that question. I believe behind the question is the belief that kids in wheelchairs are fragile.

When Aaron was three and he asked me to remove those tip casters, we made the decision then to take some risks. He couldn't walk. We were not about to tell him he couldn't play. It was not a hard decision. It was obvious to us, even back then, that if we tried to stop him we wouldn't win.

Wheelz

People have tried to give us credit for our son's accomplishments. The thing I think we did well was stay out of his way. Someday some kid following Aaron will get really hurt. Someday some surfer will be attacked by a shark, some football player will die on the field, and some baseball player will get hit in the face with a pitch. Oh, wait, those things have all happened and none of us are concluding we ought to shut down sports. We all agree life has risks, and my son found his life by taking some.

A letter from a concerned mom helps make this point.

Dear Kaylene,

I saw the interviews with your family, and your part in those touched me and made me realize how much my anxiety was affecting Claire and her sister. I realized that if you could allow Aaron to do the kind of things that he does, I could certainly let go and allow Claire to do the minor things she had been asking of me. I still remind myself of that almost every day. I've been able to see the effects of letting her go and enjoy her life rather than constantly worrying about what is going to happen to her physically. Her confidence is growing, and she is glowing again.

Brandy Persons

Aaron encourages taking risks, but he doesn't suggest anyone be reckless. He insists on helmets. The chairs are heavy and the concrete is unyielding. He has coached many children. He does a lot of flatland stunts to show they don't have to be at a skate park to play around. Aaron stresses the need to live on two wheels. For the kids, the experience is always the same—they float, they fly, they have fun, they learn to love being on a chair.

Blake is now doing a lot with track and field and basketball. That kid has an attitude I've seen before. Aaron envisioned a time when wheelchair athletes competed against each other. Thus he was more than willing to train anyone who asked.

Aaron's first public appearance with *Nitro* was in Brisbane, Australia. On May 2nd, 2010, a few days before the Brisbane shows, Aaron landed the backflip on his second try in practice. He no longer had the luxury of a foam pit. Hit or miss, he landed on the ramps.

Later that night Travis Pastrana shook his hand and said, "You crushed it today!"

Aaron couldn't get over Travis even talking to him, let alone praising him. He was even more blown away by the fact that they were on the same team.

He would say, "I'm waiting for my dreams to catch up with my life."

But while Wheelz was enjoying a life better than his dreams, his mom still had to manage it. She was tired of being overwhelmed. Just arainging wheels to send to Australia, (Aaron was bending them in every show) took monumental effort to coordinate. She desparetely needed help. She had to find an agent. That she did is a story of its own.

Agent Mom

Aaron signed a contract with a Coca-Cola distributor out of Italy in September 2009. They paid him well but we almost immediately realized that it was a mistake. They owned him worldwide for all beverage promotions for two years. No sooner had Aaron signed on the dotted line than a company in Sweden wanted him to do a chocolate drink ad, but his contract wouldn't let him.

The Italian company representing Coke sent their media group out to film Aaron for a European ad. We had them over for dinner a few nights in a row. They told us they were not used to "celebrities" doing that. Celebrities sounded so weird. We figured that they had to eat and we enjoyed their company. It was also cool to brag to my friends that we had a couple Italians, a Swede, and a few Germans over for dinner. We felt so cosmopolitan but the great thing was that we became fast friends.

When it came time to leave, a few of them took Kaylene aside and said, "You need to get Aaron an agent." The message wasn't lost on us. It was their kind way of saying, "You didn't charge enough for that contract."

Three years earlier, after the backflip, Kaylene had searched extensively for an agent. But no one knew what to do with him, so we were always turned away. We had no clue what a company like Coca-Cola was willing to pay for an advertisement, let alone a two-year exclusive contract. It could have been anywhere from 10,000 dollars to 100,000 dollars. That was too big of a margin of ignorance, so after that film crew left she started looking for an agent again.

Kaylene searched the Internet, found about ten agents, and sent out resumes with photos. That did no good. Nothing did any good until she found Shantal Lamalas.

Shantal loved sports. She played soccer in high school and for her club at UCLA. She competed in three-day eventing on the equestrian circuit. However, Shantal was more of an academic than an athlete. When she learned that there was a degree in Sports Management, she knew what field she wanted to pursue.

After six years of college and a couple of years working for a professional team, Shantal was recruited by Yee and Dubin, a sports agency and consulting firm. They represented the likes of New England Patriots quarterback Tom Brady and New Orleans Saints head coach Sean Payton.

With her experience in the sports world, Shantal had no desire to be a sports agent. She had heard too many stories of people who were willing to cross the line to win an athlete. Some agents worked in gray areas. Some were downright dishonest. She wanted no part of either.

A friend who'd known Donald Yee for twenty-plus years told her, "I wouldn't steer you wrong. Don is not like those corrupt agents. Indeed, he has turned down offers because he didn't agree with their practices. I think you'll enjoy working with him because he's not your typical agent."

With that recommendation Shantal made the leap and was glad she did. Her friend was right; Don wasn't a cheat. She was proud to play for a team that was willing to lose clients and a lot of money rather than compromise their integrity.

Kaylene's brother Leland was an accountant for a professional athlete. When Kaylene voiced her frustrations about finding an agent for Aaron, Leland said he'd talk to his client. When he asked him if he had any suggestions, his client's answer was instantaneous: "Oh, yeah, Yee and Dubin. Give them a call."

That recommendation gave Kaylene the courage to make a cold call. Luckily Shantal answered.

"Okay, I'll get to the point," Kaylene began. "My son does backflips in a wheelchair."

Shantal stared into space, trying to picture what she just heard. "Your son does what?"

"He does tricks and stunts at skate parks, including backflips. He tours with *Nitro Circus*. He's really pretty good. He gets so many requests to participate in so many things, and it's all over my head. If a magazine wants a photo, I don't know what to charge."

It was quiet on the other end of the line. Kaylene took a breath and continued, "If Coke Zero wants to do a deal I have no idea what I'm doing. I don't know the numbers. He should be protected and I have no clue how to do that. I need help."

"Okay, that makes sense." But she was thinking, *She's got a son in a wheelchair doing flips?* Still on the phone with Kaylene, Shantal was Googling Aaron on her computer and thinking, *Who is this kid?*

She told Kaylene she'd get back to her. Kaylene hung up with little hope, assuming it would be just another rejection. Why would anyone take this kid on?

After the call, Shantal talked to Carter Chow, one of the managing partners. He was surprisingly encouraging. Shantal agreed because she liked a challenge and because there was something about this story that made her want to learn more. This kid would definitely be different than any of her other clients.

She went to Don. Ultimately it was his decision because she would be spending a lot of time on this kid called "Wheelz." They knew there wouldn't be a lot of money in this client compared to professional football players, and Kaylene was not only asking for an agent to negotiate contracts, but also for a manager to schedule his appointments and manage his life.

Don said, "If you want to take this on feel free to do it."

Shantal had Don's approval but she was still not sure. She talked to her dad about it. "I'm not too familiar with what he does. I realize it's going to take a lot of time, but it might be good to learn about an area I know nothing about."

Her dad said, "If Don's giving you the go ahead, and if you want to do it, go for it."

Shantal set up a meeting with Kaylene, Aaron, and Carter Chow. They met at an Italian restaurant—Aaron's request.

When an agent courts a player it must be like dating. If the guy or girl has high standards and the other does not, it's not a good match. An athlete who wouldn't take money under the table would be attracted to an agency who wouldn't offer it. As a small agency Yee and Dubin had little overhead. Consequently, they only needed to sign a few players a year. When they court a client they naturally look for compatibility. Professional athletes are by nature proud, and having agents who want to represent them must be flattering. Agents expect ego. But to be in the Yee & Dubin family, character matters.

The young man Shantal watched eating fettuccine alfredo across the table was humbly asking her to be his agent. She was attractive. She was smart. She had the physical appearance of a fit soccer player. Notwithstanding she was also kind, Aaron found that intimidating. That turned out to play to his advantage. Shantal could tell he had a strong character, but he was also refreshingly shy. She could tell he was not only an inspiration for kids in wheelchairs, but he was also an inspiration, period.

At the end of the meeting she said, "You know what? Let me take this on. I still need to talk to my boss but I think he'll be on board with this."

She reported to Don. She told him she wanted to see where this all would lead, and that it was more than a project—it was a cause.

Don said, "Go for it."

So Shantal called Kaylene back and said, "We want to work with you."

Kaylene had that feeling you have when the elephant that has been sitting on you for three years decides to sit somewhere else. Kaylene had fully disclosed what the elephant was like. Shantal thought she knew what she was getting into. She had no clue.

Within no time, her phone and emails began blowing up on Sunday afternoons. That became the new start of her work week. Her new client was getting requests from all over the world and from places where their Monday mornings were her Sunday afternoons. That was never much of a problem with her American football players.

She was managing his schedule, negotiating his contracts, and dealing with the flood of paperwork. If Shantal wanted a

Wheelz

challenge, she got one. She would spend more time on Wheelz by far than any of her other clients. It was fun for her to be a part of his career, but it was overwhelming. Kaylene, on the other hand, could finally breathe.

By the middle of 2010 Shantal started to take over. After a few years, though, the *Nitro* management was asking Aaron to get rid of her. "We can work directly with you. We don't like Shantal."

It wasn't lost on Aaron what that meant--she was a keeper. She would say, "If they ask you to do something and you have to tell them no, blame it on me." She had no problem being the bad guy for her clients. He grew to love his agent.

Unit Clothing of Australia wanted to sponsor Aaron. Kaylene turned their request over to Shantal with the click of a forward button. That agent stuff was wonderful.

A Double Backflip

The video announcing his double backflip begins with him on the phone. It was a real call.

"Hey, Mom, guess what? I just landed the first double backflip on a wheelchair."

It was 8:29 pm on August 26th, 2010, at Woodward in Pennsylvania.

Aaron loves me. He knows I'm proud of him. I always eventually get a call. On this video he's on the phone with me as well. But he always calls his mom first. I'm kept up to date by reading emails, Instagrams, and texts he sends to her. On this, his most significant accomplishment, she was rightfully the first to know.

In the video, Aaron said he had to be relaxed and calm to do the flip. He also said, "Holding on to that bungee is anything but calming."

He used a sixty foot bungee cord to get the speed he needed. A couple of guys would pull him back and let him go like a slingshot. His first try bent an axel plate. It was immediately discouraging. He had to get the part overnighted.

He recalled, "I spent seventy bucks on that. But it was the best seventy bucks I ever spent."

Aaron had previously tried the double on his Australian tour several times. He'd tried and failed for a week just months earlier at Woodward in California.

He practiced most of the week with the foam pit. He had his heavy chair strapped around his waist. He dove in, often headfirst, with that chair and sixty--foot bungee momentum, spinning as hard as he could into that pit. Then he would unbuckle himself, pull himself out with a rope, and pull out his chair with no use of his legs. Like his first backflip, he did that about fifty times before he even tried the flip on the rezi.

On Thursday night Aaron tried and failed so much that the people at Woodward begged him to stop. He finally did stop, but only because he broke something else. He went down to his apartment to get a part. He was so tired and so discouraged he just lay on the floor and decided to quit. The thought of even making the trek back up to the practice ramps was overwhelming. It was uphill and he was exhausted. But he was running out of days. As he lay there he thought, *What am I doing? I've got to land that thing.* He figured he would never forgive himself if he gave up.

When he got to the ramps, many people had left. It was late. He tried and failed and tried and failed again. He was trying to land it

Wheelz

on the rezi, so every time he crashed his 25-pound chair would smash him. Often, he hit flat on his back and then his chair landed flat on him. Finally, one of the Woodward pros said, "That's enough. You're done." Aaron begged him for one last attempt.

Part of his motivation was that Travis had landed a double backflip on a motorcycle. He once wrote to his mom, on a different issue, "WWTPD? What Would Travis Pastrana Do?" He would keep trying.

Once again, a couple guys pulled him back, stretching the bungee held tight in his hands. Once again they let him go. He had to throw the bungee to the side then concentrate on getting the tightest tuck and the fastest rotation. He gave it all he had. He spun once; he spun again; he landed squarely on all fours.

It took a moment to sink in. He hadn't crashed. He'd landed it.

The thought that he'd been so close to giving up disturbed him. After he talked to his mom he called me.

I asked, "Is it dangerous?"

He responded, "Is it dangerous?" and just laughed.

After I saw the video that included his failed attempts, I realized how stupid that question was.

Wheelz

Aaron had already had a number of videos go viral. When he got home, he showed us the video made by Dave Metty, Brandon Schmidt, and Joshua Zucker. I knew this one would go viral, too. I tried to convince him to put one of those annoying ads at the beginning. I heard people get a few cents every time someone clicks on their video. I figured he could make a bunch of money. To his credit, he was insulted by the suggestion. He had done what no one in this world had ever done. All he wanted was to make that public. He had no clue how easy that would be.

He first appeared on MSNBC in what they called "Off the CHARTS." It was September 13th, 2010. On the same day, Aaron was interviewed in like manner with CNN. *ABC News* interviewed him on October 15th, 2010. The questions and responses were similar.

From their article I quote: "'A lot of people think of the wheelchair as a medical instrument,' Aaron told *ABC News*, as he sat among a pile of busted wheels in the backyard of his family's home. 'I think that's wrong. You know, why not think of it as something fun?'"

A few days after these interviews, Kaylene was shopping at Walmart. Aaron called and said, "Mom, do you want to go to New York?"

She asked, "What do you mean, New York?"

Aaron said, "I'm flying to New York in two hours to be on *Today*, and they just asked if you would come, too. The car service said they would be here in one hour."

Kaylene ditched her cart full of groceries. The next thing she knew, they were on a plane headed for New York. They didn't get there until 11:00 pm. They had to be to the studio at 6:00 am.

They ironed her shirt and put make-up on both of them. The two of them went into the green room and waited. Aaron and Kaylene first were interviewed outside with all of the people waving to the cameras. Then they brought Aaron into the studio.

This was undoubtedly the biggest media event to this point in Aaron's career, and yet there is little to tell. The interview was like all the others. The questions were basically the same. Those remote interviews are difficult. Live on Today was easier. They asked Kaylene to be interviewed in the studio, as well.

She said, "No – this is Aaron's thing."

Meredith Vieira said, "Chicken!" like an old friend. That was Kaylene's best part of the experience. If she has her say, she says nothing.

After the show, they went to Central Park. Aaron got a flat tire.

On February 1, 2011, Aaron's Nike commercial aired on ABC's *Primetime* right after the Super Bowl. *Nitro*'s New Zealand tour began the next day.

A Front Flip

With the double backflip accomplished, Wheelz now wanted to do a front flip. He had told me months earlier he wanted to try one. The backflip is natural off the ramp. Your momentum can flow easily into a backflip. But a front flip requires you to go against that momentum in the opposite direction. Anyone who has watched a motorcycle or BMX front flip knows it is twice as hard. All I could envision was Aaron's diving into the gap.

I said to him, "All I ask is that you get Travis's opinion. He'll understand the math." I'm sure he talked to him before he tried it.

In Auckland, New Zealand, Aaron didn't land anything squarely. But in Wellington, on February 9th, 2011, he made history. The *Nitro* announcer, with a cool Australian accent, introduced him by saying "You know what, folks? Out here at the *Nitro Circus* we have moments of absolute insanity. We have moments of absolute pure inspiration. You're about to meet one of the most, if not the most, inspiring member of the *Nitro Circus* crew. Cast your eyes to the big screen."

On the monitor they showed what Aaron could do at skate parks. Then Wheelz flew down the ramp. His rotation was perfect. He landed the backflip squarely.

He was so thrilled he begged his bosses to go again--to try a front flip. Aaron crawled up the ramp again, dragging his chair behind him. Kaylene was there. The *Nitro* bosses were happy to have her come. That evening they let her be on the stadium floor with the team to watch her boy.

As Aaron climbed those steps, visualizing what he figured would be the perfect rotation, she stood by the huge cushions at the end of the run. The announcer told the crowd Wheelz was going to attempt a front flip.

The crowd went wild. "Wheelz, Wheelz, Wheelz!" they chanted.

Aaron sucked in their energy. Before he dropped in, he raised his arms then lowered them as if worshiping the ramp gods. In reality, he was visualizing what he would need to do to get his rotation.

He dropped in. When he started up the end of the ramp, he lifted his arms over his head. When he hit the end of the ramp, he threw his arms forward, rotated just right, and nailed it.

The crowd erupted. They had witnessed the first front flip in a wheelchair. And it was beautiful.

The *Nitro* team swarmed him. But to his everlasting credit he ignored them. He rolled past them looking for his mom. When he found her she grabbed his helmet on both sides of his face and looked directly into his eyes.

On the program *Courage in Sports,* she reported, "I started to cry. I could see the athletes crying. There was screaming, jumping. He passed his way through the crowd. He looks into my face, and we both are just crying."

I'm not sure Aaron will ever appreciate what that meant to her. It was the right thing for him to do, but it was also the natural thing for him to do.

VIDEO 6: The front flip

http://goo.gl/NMUYhg

After the Melbourne show Kaylene received the following post on Facebook.

> Oh, Kaylene, it was amazing. The effect he has had on Paddy is quite overwhelming. The next morning Paddy got up and made himself breakfast & made his lunch (a first) then began to dress himself & get ready to go to the skate park. He should have been getting ready for school, but
>
> Wheelz

we took a very quick trip to the park on the way. And he's done this every morning since meeting Aaron. He's barely spoken a sentence without "Aaron" or "Wheelz" in it. Actually he's calmed down a little; it's probably only every third sentence now. A fire has been lit in Paddy to try much harder now to be independent. It's been unreal to see. But I do want to say thank you to you, Kaylene. I'm sure you are familiar with the effect Aaron has on many kids in chairs. He is someone very special & I'm sure you must be a very special mum as well. Thanks.

MGM Grand

One day on my way to work, I saw a video of *Nitro Circus* and my boy on the giant TV monitor at the MGM Grand. I think he had said something about doing a show there, but it hadn't sunk in until that moment. Kaylene hates the Las Vegas Strip because she hates crowds. She grew up in Vegas so it holds no charm for her. I cross the Strip twice a day to go to and from work. It means little to me as well. But when my son was on the monitor of one of the largest, most famous hotels in the world, it was kind of cool.

The night of the show was my first time seeing Aaron live on the Giganta Ramp.

Aaron had practiced his front flip without landing it all week. Now, before a crowd of 16,000, which included his friends and family, he needed to land it, especially because they were filming the show for the *Nitro Circus* movie.

Halfway through the show, they had a small break, and then it was Aaron's turn. They started by showing him at the top of the ramp, then they showed a brief video clip about him. I was surprised to see Kaylene and me on the screen.

It was smart to show the video because it showed what he did at skate parks, so no one could conclude the ramp was all he could do.

When Travis says, "He gets a bigger ovation," I couldn't appreciate that until that moment. It was so surreal. The emotion in the room surprised me. I have no problem being moved to tears, but I was tearing up merely because the room was filled with energy. And that was before he had even attempted the jump. The crowd, already at a fever pitch, took it up a notch, chanting, "Wheelz, Wheelz, Wheelz," in perfect cadence.

When I'd seen him in the past on video, it was always in slow motion, so I was surprised how fast he shot down that ramp in real life. There is no shame in not landing a stunt. Many had tried and failed that night. It's actually a good thing because no one takes for granted it's an easy thing. But when the athlete lands it, everyone is happy. And this time, in front of a very hopeful and supporting crowd, Aaron landed it perfectly. If I thought the emotion and noise had reached its apex, I had to think again. Never in my life have I heard such a large crowd so united in one elated feeling.

My wife had said, in one interview, "You see videos and you see YouTube; he talks about performing in front of these huge crowds, but until you see it in person, you don't really get it."

That announcer in New Zealand said it was "pure inspiration," and indeed it was. At the end of the show, they had a finale. BMXers and skateboarders went down the ramp in rapid succession. To our surprise, Aaron was among them. It happened so quickly it took a moment to realize he was trying another stunt. When he hit the gap, he attempted a double backflip. He got the rotation right, but his chair tilted sideways. He landed on his side and didn't get up.

His sister Lisa bolted from her seat. The security guards tried to stop her from going onto the main floor, but she said, "That's my brother. You can't stop me." They let her in.

Kaylene and I couldn't get past them. No one ever does, but Lisa. Aaron was in tremendous pain. He didn't dare move his right arm. After the show, he was pushed up the top of the landing ramp. He waved to the fans, suggesting he was okay, but he wasn't.

Kaylene took him to the emergency room for X-rays. They took forever to attend to him. Thankfully, it was just bruised ribs. All in all, it had been a wonderful night. In a way, it almost seemed poetic that it ended with Aaron and his mom spending the night, sitting next to each other, in a hospital. The X-rays showed he hadn't broken anything, but he was bruised and sore.

-The next day we picked up his truck at the hotel. He asked me to throw his chair in the back because he was in considerable pain.

Wheelz

When he got home, he got his chair out and we never heard about any pain again. I guess he figured it was part of the deal. The next week, he was scheduled for a photo shoot wherein he was supposed to perform at the skate park. He was concerned he would be in too much pain to do it. When the time came he was still sore, but he did the shoot without much of a problem.

Life Rolls On

After Aaron won the BMX Advanced on October 25th, 2008, he could no longer compete. About that time Am Jams came to an end. It all seems like a dream. There was this wonderful season of opportunity for my boy to progress and compete in the only extreme sport series in America at the time. Joe Wichert did not create the parks or Am Jam for my son, but it seems like he did. Aaron wouldn't compete again for three years.

With the help of his family, Jesse Billauer established *Life Rolls On* after a spinal cord injury resulted in paralysis. I once asked him how depressed he was when he woke up and found he was a quadriplegic. He said he figured that was life and he needed to move on. The organization he founded reflected that attitude. They sponsored a yearly event called Life Rolls On: They Will Surf Again. They provided opportunities for kids with spinal injuries to go surfing. It was quite successful.

In 2011, Jesse and his group wanted to sponsor Life Rolls On: They Will Skate Again. They enlisted the help of Superman. On May 27th, 1995, Christopher Reeve, star of the 1978 movie *Superman*, was thrown from a horse and became a quadriplegic. He required a wheelchair and breathing apparatus for the rest of his life. He and his wife Dana championed many causes on behalf of people with spinal-cord injuries. They founded the Christopher and Dana Reeve Foundation.

Life Rolls On and the Christopher and Dana Reeve Foundation set up a day (July 29th, 2011) to teach kids in wheelchairs how to play at skate parks. That was to be followed by a Wheelchair Motocross (WCMX) competition. Aaron had changed the name of the sport from Hardcore Sitting to WCMX. He thought it described the sport better.

Six years after his fist appearance on *The Stefan Raab Show* Aaron was invited back again.. Stefan asked, "So is this a special Hardcore Sitting wheelchair?"

Aaron: "Yeah, well, WCMX wheelchairs, Wheelchair Motocross like BMX." He was still focused on his goal.

Life Rolls On wanted Aaron to coach and compete.

They told Aaron they assumed he would win. When he heard first prize was five-thousand dollars, he was more than happy to help out. When Aaron got to Venice Beach, California, where the event was to take place, he was amazed at the number of people, mainly young kids, who showed up in wheelchairs. Aaron loved helping the kids at the park. To see the thrill of a child going down his or her first ramp--to see them grasp the possibilities--is rewarding, to say the least.

The kids on skateboards gave Wheelz some competition. Some kids get pretty good on skateboards with prosthetic legs, but Aaron did win. Five thousand dollars was a huge prize. For their money, Life Rolls On claimed the honor of sponsoring the first WCMX competition, albeit mixed, with skateboarders. More importantly, they inspired a group of kids to see their chairs as a piece of equipment in a sport.

The word was getting out. As proof of this, *Glee* wanted Aaron in another episode (February 2012). This time his stunts were to be at a skate park. The episode had Artie and a girl on a wheelchair at a skate park as if that's what kids on wheelchairs do. They wanted Aaron to go down a simple ramp. Again they paid him well. And millions watching that episode saw kids on wheelchairs playing at a skate park portrayed as a natural part of American culture.

At the same time, AT&T paid a lot of money to use the phrase "Hardcore Sitting" in conjunction with "WCMX" in their ads. Also at this time the Guinness people invited him to Italy to set a third record. They didn't know what they were going to have him do; they just wanted him back on the show. This time, I went.

Aaron wanted to set the record for longest distance on one wheel. They wanted him to do the most spins in a wheelchair in one minute. That's what he did, so he got another record. Aaron thought little of the record, but we did get an all-expense-paid trip to Italy.

Wheelz

The second year (2012) of Life Rolls On: They Will Skate Again, we decided to go watch. It was moving to watch him and others help the kids. There were a lot of kids in wheelchairs smiling.

Aaron had always wanted some competition, and this year, he had it. This year, it wasn't a foregone conclusion he would win. The problem was they once again included skateboarders in the event.

Those skateboarders were good. It's like I said about that X Games exhibition: people take for granted what they've accomplished. That got Aaron a lot of attention in that exhibition. Now, it was coming back to haunt him. In our hotel that evening, Aaron told me he wasn't sure he could beat those guys. I admitted they looked good.

I said, "Did you notice all those wheelchair kids at the skate park today? Did you notice most of them were wearing full face helmets. For years, I only knew of one kid who wore a full face helmet at skate parks, and that was you. I hope you win. I think you will. But if not, what I saw today is enough. This is becoming a sport. Win or lose, they can't take that away from you."

I'm not sure if that helped or hurt. He could have thought, *Great — how would it look if the pioneer of this sport lost?*

When the competition began, it was clear that Evan Strong (who would go on to be a Paralympics gold medalist) would be his main competition. He had been at the X Games with Aaron. What a cool name – "Strong." Aaron's birth name was Tony. We changed it to "Aaron" because it meant "strength" or "mountain of strength." So on this day, it would be strong versus strength.

In WCMX, BMX, and skater competitions, every competitor waits while one performs for about a minute and a half. Judges stand around the park making notes on their clipboards. It had been years since I had seen Aaron compete. He was always the only one on a wheelchair. I wondered if he would get any competition from the wheelchair group.

I was surprised how good some of the WCMXers were. One kid rode a grinding bar and dropped onto a table to shorten his fall. Aaron told me he was tempted to do it without the table, but he didn't want to upstage that kid. Other kids dropped down the ten-foot ramp, through the bowl, and up seven or so feet the other side.

But I was surprised when Aaron did his run. He began by dropping into that ten-foot bowl and shooting up the other side. He did his handplant and shot down for another trick. After that one trick I realized I was watching a pro.

Then Evan Strong took his turn. He looked every bit the pro as well.

Everyone did their runs. The time ran out. But the announcer told Aaron and Evan to keep going. Aaron tried to rise high enough above that ten-foot wall to do a backflip, but he came short about two inches. Each time, his front wheels caught the coping. He caught himself at the top, slapping his arms on the flat surface, keeping himself from falling back into the bowl.

Evan flew off that ten-foot ledge and tried to land on his skateboard. He could land on it but not stay on it. They must have each tried their respective tricks ten to twelve times. Aaron tried to thrust himself just a little harder to get the height he needed. Evan kept trying to stay up on the landing.

Strong versus strength, it was like two gladiators fighting to the death. The crowd knew it was a legitimate duel. Finally, Evan busted his board and the competition was over. We did not know who the winner would be. Had either landed their trick, it would have been a foregone conclusion.

After they announced third place, we waited in suspense. Then they announced Evan Strong in second place. We were obviously thrilled for Aaron and celebrated at his favorite restaurant: Olive Garden, his treat.

The MegaRamp

Later in the year we were invited to the *Nitro Circus* movie premiere. I was surprised by the movie. It was a documentary about great stuntmen with a bit of a storyline. It was better than I thought it would be. It had a great beginning with some dirt buggies and about three dozen motorcycles flying crisscross in a giant panorama. The 3D was cool. The humor was good.

The stunts throughout the movie were wild but not stupid. In fairness to the reader, I won't tell the story. I will say that they honored my son by making him an inspirational part of the movie. They honored him even more by equating his achievements with Travis' childhood dreams.

Nitro Circus did a European tour. At some of the stadiums there were whole rows of kids on wheelchairs. Aaron was knocked unconscious in England. It was such a bad wreck that *Nitro* started replaying it as part of Wheelz's intro. He said funny things when he came to, arguing politics with an English paramedic.

After the show he sat in the locker room alone for the longest time, hurting. As he came out, there was a kid on a wheelchair with his dad. They had waited for Aaron after the crowd had gone. Aaron talked to him for a while, then asked him if he would like his helmet. Aaron was not going to use the helmet again, since he'd hit it so hard, but he hangs on to all his old helmets like he keeps his old chairs. With a splitting headache that would disorient him for a couple days, he knew that kid would appreciate that helmet more than he would. Of course, the boy was thrilled.

I've thought of that boy often. I think I know what he thinks of Aaron. I imagine that helmet sitting on a dresser in his room. For me, it is a sweet thought. Movie premieres are cool, but I'm proudest to be his dad at moments like that.

At other moments, Aaron is anything but a hero. He gets angry—sometimes over the littlest things. If someone interrupts him while he's talking at the dinner table, he may not say anything, but he tightens a fist.

We went to a diner one night to get some ice cream. The host tried to remove a chair so Aaron could stay on his wheelchair. Aaron likes to sit on regular seats at the table.

When the guy left he said, "I hate when everyone tries to help you when you don't need help."

I said, "I once asked a guy at Carl's Jr., standing at the counter with crutches and a tray if he wanted any help. He responded in great anger."

Aaron said, "I don't want to talk about this."

I said, "I'm just saying, 'We may be stupid, but we're well-meaning.'"

"I don't want to talk about this."

"All I'm saying is there is another perspective, and I'll add that I've never seen you voice your anger to those people."

Aaron got in his chair and left the restaurant. I texted him and said, "Let's just talk about this," but he wouldn't hear it. To be fair, his rolling away is his way of avoiding a fight, but I hate it because offering a contrary view is nowhere close to a fight and having it interpreted as such is disconcerting.

As much as we both dislike such encounters, tomorrow is another day and we understand that. The next morning we laughed and joked and went forward as if nothing had happened.

Later that day he said, "I transferred five bucks to your account for that hot fudge sundae."

When he was young, he used to punch my walls. I say "my" because I'm the one who always had to patch them. I got good at that. With his strong upper body strength, those walls had no chance. Some have suggested his anger may stem from being Italian. Kaylene and I believe that totally.

Wheelz

He once told us that he saw his biological dad get so angry and thought, *That's where I get it.*

There was one guy on a wheelchair who hated Aaron. They were once friends. But the guy's resentment increased as Aaron's success increased. They both disliked each other immensely. One time, his old nemesis said something rude to him at Walmart, so Aaron pushed him. It didn't hurt him at all; it merely made him go a little faster. Nevertheless, he called the police. The Walmart video camera showed the push. The guy pressed charges. Aaron got a ticket. He went to court, had to pay a fine, and had to take an anger management course.

On the walls going down to his room, my wife placed some of his awards. Next to his Medal of Honor, Aaron placed his certificate for completing his "Impulse Control Program." I guess he wanted to put all of his awards from the city in the same area.

That certificate is official documentation Aaron is human. I assumed he would be resentful of the fine and class. I figured it would make him angry. Actually he was grateful for the lesson. He said he learned some helpful strategies. He didn't put it on the wall because he's proud of it; he wanted the reminder of what his anger cost him.

With that anger came great passion. His determination was not for show. He would work on a trick, and no matter how bruised or battered he got, he wouldn't stop until he mastered it. Landing his double backflip is but one example.

When Aaron and his mom went to Italy to set his second Guinness World Record, they wanted him to do a flip over a bar for a height record. He hit his head hard about three times. They asked him to stop. Then they asked my wife to get him to stop.

She said, "The reason he's here is because he doesn't stop."

They finally convinced him the height record would be better to set without the flip. He set the record because he was the first to set any height record.

Before *Nitro Circus*, Aaron thought his only chance at a MegaRamp was with Bob Burnquist. Bob is one of the greatest skateboarders in the world. He is popularly known as "Big Bob Burnquist." In the skateboard world, he is huge. For the Summer X Games, he's earned twelve gold, six silver, and seven bronze medals.

John Lytle tried to get Aaron and Bob together years earlier without success. After Aaron was with *Nitro*, Bob invited him to "Burnquist's Dreamland." That is what he calls his backyard, which has the longest ramp in the world. The ramp is about 360 feet long. It is seventy-five feet at the top of the ramp. It has a 180-foot roll-in to a ramp that launches people across a seventy-foot gap. Bob's ramp also has a fifty-five-foot-tall platform leading to a 50-foot gap. The landing is a twenty-seven-foot ramp that leads to a thirty-foot quarterpipe that can launch a rider high into the air.

Bob wanted to do a documentary of Wheelz going down that ramp. Aaron was thrilled to hang out with Bob and play in his backyard, but when he saw the ramp, which was about five feet higher than Nitro's, with a ten-foot wider gap, he had second thoughts.

He said in the documentary, "That thing's scary. What have I got myself into?"

On top of the ramp he said, "Oh my gosh! This is Bob's Dreamland. What's wrong with Bob's dreams?"

If you crash on the down ramp after the gap you slide to the bottom. Usually that's no big deal. But at the top of the ramp is about five feet of flat surface. The turn from that surface to the down ramp is called the knuckle. You don't want to land on either.

On Aaron's first time down he landed on the knuckle and hurt his back, but he was okay. He needed more speed. So they built the

Wheelz

ramp about eight feet higher. Months earlier he had busted parts of his two front teeth at Woodward. He had them glued back on. On his second attempt down Burnquist's ramp he hit the knuckle again. Again he busted them out.

Bob asked him if he wanted to go again. He proposed he follow Wheelz down the ramp on his skateboard and give him a push for added speed. Aaron agreed. He crashed again, but on the down slope, so he was fine, and done.

In the documentary Bob said, "That is the best part. That is the reason why I keep skating. Wheelz is inspiring. He's crazy, gnarly, he kept at it. I mean, he lost his teeth and went again. That's just unheard of. I'd want to be out of there. Lots of times, it's like 99 percent bailing and getting hurt and one percent glory. I'm ready to go out there and learn every trick possible and not complain. But, uh, he's got to fix himself, so a quick trip to the dentist. He lives to ride another day." Then they rode off in a helicopter.

VIDEO 7: Bob Burnquist's Dreamland
http://goo.gl/pBw3y9

We didn't know why Aaron wanted to go down that ramp, other than that it was Bob Burnquist's, but we later learned he had another ramp in mind. He was at Bob's to practice for a much scarier ramp: the MegaRamp in Brazil.

On the way to the airport at the end of August of 2012, I asked Aaron, "Where you going?"

"Brazil."

"Why Brazil?"

"To do the MegaRamp."

"I thought you do the MegaRamp with *Nitro*."

"No, that's the Giganta Ramp. They're not allowed to legally call it the MegaRamp. The MegaRamp is in Brazil. It is about twenty feet higher than *Nitro*'s ramp."

"Are you scared?"

"Yeah. Shantal thinks I'm crazy because they're not paying me enough. I practiced on Bob Burnquist's ramp to prepare but didn't do too well there. So yeah, I'm scared. The thing that really worries me is wheel wobble."

"Wheel wobble?"

"Yeah, that ramp is so high and so steep if I get going too fast my front wheels can start to wobble. That can slow me down or throw me off course, and that could be bad."

"So how do you know if your wheels will wobble?"

"You don't until you're halfway down the ramp. By then if they wobble there's nothing you can do about it."

"Well, I hope they don't wobble."

"Me too."

I was now agreeing with Shantal--this was crazy. In an interview with Keith Hamm, Aaron talked about his experience with Bob Burnquist.

He said, "I just destroyed a wheel, but I survived. I didn't really do too well at your house; like, how am I going to do in Brazil? So I bought a mouth guard, packed my bags, and left for Brazil. I see the ramp, and I'm like, 'Oh, that's tall.'"

The picture from his helmet cam shows that the ramp is straight down. It looks like riding down the face of a seven-story office building.

Wheelz

I get scared just looking at the picture. Aaron was scared spitless, but he went over the edge and down the ramp. His wheels did not wobble. He flew off the ramp fifty to sixty feet into the air. His arms were outstretched like an airplane. He churned them wildly to keep his chair upright and square. He wasn't about to try a backflip; he just wanted to safely land that thing. With all due respect to those BMXers, landing with two large wheels on the front and back of their bikes must be easier than what Wheelz has to do. He has such a short wheel base, and those two front skateboard wheels don't allow much room for error.

In an interview made by MegaRamp, Aaron talked about his experience: "Well, the MegaRamp and I don't have the best history. I've always had a lot of on-and-off types of situations, and then I was like, 'Oh, great, I'm going to Brazil to knock my teeth out again.' That was pretty much what I was thinking. I just kind of shred the quarter a bit just to make sure my chair was going good so I would know what to do with the quarter when I got there.

"The way I thought about it this time was instead of worrying so much about making the gap like I always do, I was just kind of thinking like, 'Maybe if I think past the gap, if I think about the quarter, then I'll make the gap.'

I come out here. I'm scared to death. I get up there. I was just like, *Make sure my chair goes straight.* And once it was going straight, I was just like, *Yeah!* Then I'm in the air and I was like, *Knuckle, no!* I kind of pulled up a little bit and I barely hit the knuckle--not enough to bounce me. And then I'm going down and I just went for a handplant on the quarter, but once I made it to the quarter, it worked perfectly. I made it over the gap and I was like, *Great, now I've got to deal with the quarter, dang it.* I was, like, fist-pumping on the way to the quarter and you see me grab the wheels again and go for a handplant. I almost got coping, I was on the sticker, so I was so close."

The pros picked him up and carried him around over their shoulders. One of those pros was Bob Burnquist.

When he got home we were thrilled that he hadn't died. And we were thrilled he had landed it clean. We were also thrilled when his photo took a two-page spread in *Sports Illustrated* (September 3rd, 2012). It is now the cover of this book.

My copy of that *Sports Illustrated* issue sits atop my filing cabinet in my office at work. Any unsuspecting student that accidentally wanders into my office will most likely see that picture.

At the end of his interview about his experience, Aaron said, "One thing I learned about the MegaRamp is it is scary, scares me to death, knocks my teeth out. But you just gotta keep trying—

Wheelz

keep going at it. Keep trying because you never know how close you are if you're about to give up."

VIDEO 8: The MegaRamp

http://goo.gl/vcgkpZ

This book cannot chronical all of Aaron's experiences. The following was Aaron's schedule for the last quarter of 2012 and the beginning of 2013.

September 27th to 29th /2012 Western Kentucky University speech & demo (Friday) and Spina Bifida Assoc. of Kentucky appearance.

October 2nd/2012 Commercial Contract with Lincoln Continental filmed in Canada.

October 5th to 7th /2012 Travis Pastrana's Nitro fundraiser in Illinois.

October 8th to 16th/2012 Schwalbe Rehacare trip to Germany

October 23rd/2012 Interview for Discovery Channel Canada at the Pro park.

November 15th to December 9th:/2012 *Nitro Circus* European tour

January 23rd to February 10, New Zealand tour.

March first to June 9th, third Australian tour.

On October 10th, 2012, Aaron bought a house. We were anxious to have him move out. We love our son, but he never threw anything away. He got so many shirts and hats and shoes from sponsors. Our house was filling up. He doesn't wear out shoes. Kaylene dreamt of the day his stuff would be gone. If that included her boy leaving the nest, then that was fine.

In July 2013, Wheelz competed in the Life Rolls On event again. He had heard rumors that skateboarders and WCMXers would not have to compete against each other. It was just a rumor.

Not taking it for granted he would win, Aaron went a week ahead to practice. There is no place at that Venice Beach Park to do a backflip on a chair. It is basic math. If you can't get enough speed

Wheelz

going down, you can't go up high enough on the other end. He had proved that the year before, but he had a plan. He had done backflips at parks with kids pushing him, so he recruited some pushers. With their help, he could land it.

On the day of the competition John Lytle and Mike Box showed up. Evan Strong didn't show up. Aaron was relieved,

In the competition, Aaron saved the flip for last. That was enough for the win.

He told me afterwards, "I always feel bad when I win. It means someone had to lose. But the thought of losing is a worse feeling."

I told him that's exactly where he needed to be.

Mike's company, Box Wheelchairs, had only been going for three or four years by the 2013 Life Rolls On competition.There were dozens of kids riding wheelchairs--most of them were on Box Wheelchairs.

I once asked Mike what his secret was. He said there are actually some trade secrets he keeps to himself.

I said, "So it would be virtually impossible for anyone to break your chairs at a skate park, considering what Aaron puts them through on giant ramps."

Wheelz

He said, "Yeah, but if they did break they have a lifetime guarantee anyway."

Without Mike's chairs WCMX would be impossible. Someday, a thousand years in the future, someone will dig up a Box Wheelchair with Spinergy wheels and Schwalbe tires and go for a ride.

China Show

Nitro Circus wanted to do a couple shows in China. Aaron didn't want to go. It was a long flight, he was tired, and frankly he didn't care about the pay. *Nitro* went back and forth with him through Shantal. They finally convinced him to go. He was glad he did. Of that trip I will share only one series of texts between him and his mom.

Aaron: "Just finished the first show! Landed my front flip over the 40 first try in the show. Third front flip landed today! I have landed 5 out of 6 jumps since being here. And I got another MVC!!!"

"Wonderful, I'm happy for you."

"Another trophy for my house."

"The crowd love you???"

"So much. The best crowd I think so far! People were on their feet before I went down the ramp! They shelter wheelchair users in this country and don't let them leave the house (shame or something) so it kinda opened their eyes!!"

"That made me cry. Do you even realize what you are doing for people?!?!?

Wheelz

"Makes ya think how last minute I ended up being brought to China. . . People here needed to see this!

"I can't stop crying. Good cry."

Rebel with a Cause

On *Nitro*'s American P.R. tour Aaron got in trouble with the law in New York. Here's his Instagram post.

> Almost got arrested for going down an escalator just now. They told me I couldn't go down on my wheelchair and I insisted that I could and proceeded to get on because, well, I'm perfectly able to. And then they had the police come and everything. My friend Dorig was cursing at them in French. I was preaching the constitution . . . and missed our train. But the cops were so cool. They even let us take the escalator back up to get new tickets. I will break this "wheelchair means I can't do anything" stereotype before I die.

Shantal went on the tour to keep people from talking Aaron into doing backflips. He was at one stake park wherein he couldn't help himself. Here is the text conversation between Aaron and his mom on September 27th, 2013.

"I thought you weren't going to flip. Then I see on FB you flipped."

"I got in plenty of trouble, hahaha."

"From who? Shantal?"

"Yeah, haha. I couldn't help it tho."

"Was she there or just heard about it?"

"I told her. I didn't want to try to hide it from her."

"Good choice. Did she yell or guilt trip you?"

"Little lecture, haha."

"I could tell she was upset."

"Sorry, live and learn, right?"

"WWTPD?"

"I knew I was going to get into trouble. I would do it all over again. It's my career."

"Yes, it's your life."

"Yep."

"Love you, good night!"

"Good night, my boy! Love you too."

Wheelz

"Are you in a trauma hospital? Someone posted a picture of you."

"There's also quite a picture of you on Times Square with your name on the billboard."

"Cool, huh???"

"I've been visiting rehab hospitals."

"I'm going to cry again. What an amazing life you're having. Helping people all the time and making a great living too. Amazing!"

"I got to meet this kid that was a skater and got hit by a car. And I made a special visit to the hospital just to meet him. The mom said it was the first time he had smiled in 3 months... Was pretty cool."

"Wow! Like Germany."

"Better, I think!"

Mom "Ya, you could talk to this kid."

"Haha, true."

Wheelz

On October 21st, Aaron flew to Colorado for a fundraiser, skate park demo, and benefit for disabled children. During the demo Aaron was hurt trying his backflip. His sister Lisa lives in Colorado and was thrilled, like old times, to take care of him. He texted me later and said he was fine but glad to have her there.

Aaron visited with children in a school for special needs. It's not like he is thrilled to go when such visits are on his itinerary; he would rather be at a skate park. He would rather be at a skate park than tour France. He is as selfish as the rest of us. But when he gets there it's magic.

Every year Primary Children's Hospital held a spina bifida clinic wherein a number of specialists saw all the children and checked for common ailments. That meant Aaron spent many hours for many days over many years in waiting rooms with kids like himself. For him going to a clinic is like visiting old friends or attending another spina bifida camp, which he always enjoyed. He is so at home with those kids.

Lisa told me the kids climbed all over him at this clinic. The lady in charge told Lisa he seemed so comfortable with children with delayed development. She said most people are not.

I asked Aaron about it and was surprised at his answer: "There were not that many kids in wheelchairs. They just had special needs. I was comfortable with them because many of them were like Mikey."

For years we wondered why we adopted Mikey. He was such a strain on our family. Kaylene and I concluded that it was to show us how ugly we are. Before Mikey we thought we were good parents. We thought we were patient. He showed us that we were neither.

Mikey had a habit of repeatedly asking the same questions like, "What would happen if we removed a manhole cover?"

We would answer, "People would get hurt."

He would ask the question again. One time, my patience used up, I yelled at him the answer I had given a dozen times. He cried and then his nose began to bleed. I had emotionally smacked a child with a seven-year-old mental capacity. I felt like a monster.

With Aaron's travels he would run into many Mikeys. He was comfortable with them. Maybe that was why.

Nitro's second European tour began with a two-week P.R. tour. With a few of the team, managers, and Wheelz, they covered Europe from England to Russia. On October 29th, 2013, Aaron made a second appearance on *The Stefan Raab Show*. This time they had bigger ramps and Stefan played *Nitro* footage It was a vivid display of how far Aaron had come in five years. He was not nervous. He landed his backflip. It was like he was revisiting an old friend. *Nitro* could not have asked for better publicity.

Before *Nitro*'s American tour Kaylene received the following message on Facebook on December 4th, 2013:

> Hey Mrs. Fotheringham, I have a question. Do you know if Aaron will be at the *Nitro Circus Live* in Hamilton, Ontario, Canada? I will be going to the show and would just like to know if he will be there. Please let me know, thanks. Signed Phil Hotwheelz Cook.

> Kaylene responded, "I only have an older schedule, but there is a show in Hamilton on January 3rd. Is that it?"

> Phil: "Yes, that is the show."

> Kaylene: "He is scheduled to be in that show as far as I know."

> Phil: "I hope so. He is why I want to go see *Nitro Circus*. It would be awesome to meet him."

> Kaylene: "I hope it happens for you. Sometimes security makes it hard."

Phil: "True, I'm getting V.I.P. tickets. And thanks so much for the help. You will be the first one to know if I get to meet Aaron."

Kaylene: "With V.I.P. tickets you will meet him. That's great."

Phil: "It will mean everything to meet him. Not too many people know this, but seeing Aaron's backflip in 2007 saved my life. If it wasn't for me seeing that video … and I want to thank Aaron for it. He saved my life and made me see that there is a lot to life."

The day of the Canadian show, Kaylene texted Aaron about Phil's desire to meet him. Aaron said it might be difficult because the V.I.P. section was more separated from the *Nitro* team than in the past.

She said, "Okay, well, try. He really wants to meet you." She didn't say anything about saving his life, etc. On the day before the show, Phil's brother posted the following:

It's *Nitro Circus* time!!! I'm so stoked to be able to share this experience with my lil bro Phil. It's gonna be one heck of a long trip but well worth it to meet Aaron Fotheringham . . . I'll die trying to get a pic of the two of them together if I have to . . . But hoping it's not that

Wheelz

tough, lol. Can you imagine meeting your number-one idol??? That's huge. Stoked for you, lil bro!! Let's do this!!

Again, Kaylene said none of this to Aaron. She didn't want to put undue pressure on him right before a show.

About 4:00 pm Aaron texted and asked, "What does that kid look like?"

Kaylene responded, "You can't miss him. He's in a chair and he has a green and yellow Mohawk."

A little later Aaron texted back and said, "That was a sweet experience."

Evidently the V.I.Ps were separated from the *Nitro* team. The team waved at the group from the main floor then headed to the locker room to get ready for the show. They only had thirty minutes before the show started. Aaron headed through the crowd looking for Phil. It was hard because a lot of people wanted him to stop. He found Phil and his brother, and they talked and took pictures. Phil gave Aaron some Canadian candy and a Canadian flag.

After the show Phil's brother posted the following:

Wheelz

Outside of watching my children being born, tonight was one of the most amazing experiences ever. And I don't mean the crazy, death-defying insanity I observed. That was very cool, don't get me wrong. But we had almost given up on all hope of seeing Aaron up close 'cause . . well . . the wheelchair sections at Copps suck and are at the top of the lower level. And we were a long way from Aaron even though we could see him messing around on the arena floor. We had all but given up hope of getting to meet him and went on watching the show. All of the sudden someone was poking Hotwheelz in the arm. He was actually getting a bit angry when we looked over and saw Wheelz with his huge smile and a 'how's-it-goin'!! We all just about [died]!!! What a great guy!! He found us!!! I'm still in tears just thinking about it. So happy you got to meet Aaron, Phil Hotwheelz Cook Baxwar. That was awesome!!"

Aaron knows what it's like to meet your hero. He will never forget the day at the X Games when Travis waved at him. To be that for someone else is kind of cool.

When Aaron was in Salt Lake, he invited Greg Haerr (the secret millionaire) to the show. Greg was flattered and grateful. Aaron thought it was the least he could do and was thrilled to see him.

When the *Nitro* show was in Anaheim, it was Mike Box's turn to finally see Wheelz live on the Giganta Ramp. Aaron could hardly move his arm. It wasn't broken, but he was in tremendous pain from a crash the night before. Mike said he too was amazed at the electricity in the crowd for Aaron's turn. He knew Aaron was hurt and was impressed he was going on with the show regardless. It was the last show of the tour. Aaron figured he could worry about his arm afterwards. Aaron crashed again on his first attempt. He didn't want to end the tour like that, so he made one last attempt. Mike told me he was in tears witnessing Aaron's determination. Then he was in tears when he succeeded.

Aaron asked Mike to roll one of his chairs to Mike's truck. When people realized it was Wheelz's chair, they wanted to touch it. Mike said it was almost spiritual but also a little strange. They just touched it then moved on to let others do the same. It was a rewarding night for Mike. He told me he was happy to be a part of Aaron's life.

I responded, "A significant part!"

A Double Front Flip

Aaron didn't want to go to Africa. Just coming off *Nitro*'s European and American tours, he was sick of traveling. He was also sick with bronchitis.

After the tour we didn't pick Aaron up at the airport. He had asked one of his friends to do it. We were fine with that, but we usually got all the details of his travels on the ride home. When he got home he came immediately to his mom to give a full report. I was glad I was there because he had a story to tell.

The first thing Aaron realized about Africa is that it is beautiful—more so than New Zealand, which is amazing because New Zealand is gorgeous. There were about 25,000 in the stands at Cape Town.

Aaron said, "The crowds went crazy. They were awesome. They were so loud."

In that show the ramps were warm and faster than ever, so he overrotated. He did a one-and-a-half flip and realized with a little more speed he could do a double front flip.

The next show was in Durban.

Aaron was reading a book on the tour called *Hero (The Secret)* by Rhonda Byrne. He told us, "It pretty much tells you how to become a hero. I know that sounds weird, like I'm trying to become a hero, but it helps you accomplish your dreams. It talks about committing, which was really important because the double front flip takes more commitment than any trick I've done so far.

"You have to be fully committed from the top of the ramp because you're pushing into the ramp faster than you would for a single front flip, so by the time you push over the edge, you're committed because you're going too fast to do anything else. Even if you don't feel you threw it hard enough, you have to go all the way because if you open up you're going to get hurt, so you've got to just wish for the best and stay in a ball."

"The book said you need to chase what makes you happy. You have a calling in life whether it's to be a teacher or a wheelchair front flipper. At one point it talks about if you're no longer happy, if you're chasing your dream, sometimes your path shifts and it will start to feel like a job. And that's when you need to start chasing your dream again and follow what makes you happy. And sometimes that risks you quitting what you're doing and going in a whole different direction.

"It talks about how you can be risking income. That's a big one that stops people from chasing their dream because, 'Oh I'm making money right now, but I want to do this, but I'm scared to

Wheelz

leave my job because I won't make money or whatever.' And that was a concern because if I get hurt doing this double front flip then that can put me out of a job. But it's worth it to me to be happy to chase that dream than to not chase it because I want to make a paycheck."

I asked, "So *Nitro* was starting to feel like a job?"

"Yeah, I was starting to feel like it was too much of the same thing every day. Like, go to work and do a front flip. Go to work, do a front flip. And I wasn't happy anymore. So I thought I need to go to work and do a double front flip.

"Just thinking about the double the day before made me happy, the thought of trying something new and the thought if Travis was there he'd be really excited. For me I feel like my calling is to progress WCMX, and I was starting to feel like just doing a single front flip—it had been, like, 2011 when I first started doing front flips, and ever since then I hadn't done anything new. I'm at a point in my life when I'm young and I'm not really scared to get hurt, that I need to do it, to progress it as far as I can. And it's not my dream and it's not my calling to just do shows and be stagnant. I want to keep progressing. And maybe if I'm not happy doing shows I'm meant to be progressing."

As Aaron was talking, I thought of the dozens of times I told him to be content with that front flip. I had told him that even though that flip was old for him it was new for the crowd. Why risk injury when he was already inspiring the crowd? As he talked I was learning why.

"I told Cam, our manager, about the double the day before. There was a buzz going around. I'd been talking to a lot of people, probably more than I should have. I should have just kept it all to myself. But it was good to get reassurance from all that believed in me. It's good to have allies.

"That's what that book talks about too. It talks about naysayers and allies and how there are people that are going to help you and there are people that are going to discourage you. That also helped me. But I read that part after the whole attempt. I was like, 'Oh, that would have been nice.' But actually reading that book after I had gone through it, the book helped me get through all the negative part. I thought, *Well, when you're chasing your dream you're going to have people against you.*

"Before the show the energy was high. Everyone was getting ready. They announced, 'We've got ten minutes until show time.' Everyone was getting their gear on, and Cam stops me in the hallway to tell me something. I'm listening to my music, getting amped up to try a double front flip, and I'm feeling all these positive vibes, and then, boom, he says, 'You can't do a double front flip,' for whatever reason. He's like, 'We're going to save it.' He pretty much said, 'If you do it here in South Africa then the

Wheelz

next time you come here you'll have to do something bigger. You ought to save it for Australia.' I thought it was so unfair because he hadn't shut me down sooner. He just let me think that he was fine with it.

"I'd felt so confident. That's why I was so upset, because I actually believed I could do it. I landed it in my head ten times the night before, before I went to sleep. I was in bed when I was visualizing it. My eyes were wide open. I couldn't even sleep because I was so excited. Because I felt I was going to land a double front flip the next day. That's how positive I felt.

"Cam was insistent. I didn't want to hear it, so I rolled away. He doesn't know how to deal with me when I'm angry like you guys do. He doesn't know to let me alone so we can finish the discussion later. Cam's at the top of the ramp every night to direct people and tell them when to go and stuff, and right before I'm about to go, he said, "Just please promise me you're just going to do a front flip.' I didn't really give him a definite answer."

"Before my turn I saw Brandon Schmidt do a double front flip on a snowboard. He threw it and landed it perfectly. I was like, 'Oh my gosh, if he could do it,' and then I saw R. Wheely do one on a scooter. He throws it so fast that he pauses in the air between rotations then tucks into a ball and finishes it. I thought to myself, *If he can take a break in the middle of the air, stop his whole rotation and start it again, I could probably do a double front flip if I throw it as hard as I can and stay in a ball.* I visualized it a lot before I tried it.

"In that book it also says one of the keys to an athlete's success is visualizing. Like, most athletes visualize their success over and over. The book also talked about fear. It talked about how courage is built by doing things that cause you to be scared—like you're not just born fearless, you have to build it. That helped too. It said most of us are scared to follow our dreams and what stops us is fear. Fear of the unknown. Fear of not making money. Fear of failure. Then it said, but in some cases it may be physical harm they are afraid of and that applies to extreme athletes. I was like, 'Oh, it's talking right to me.' And then it just went back to talking about regular people. I thought that was cool because it actually said 'extreme athletes.' I was like, *Oh my gosh.* It felt like that book was targeted at me.

"When they announced me they asked me what I was going to do, and I said, 'Uh, I'm going to'—I kind of stuttered—'a flip.' In my mind I was thinking *double front flip*, but I couldn't say that. It was funny because afterwards everyone brought that up. They were like, 'We just knew you were going to do it.'

"Brandon Schmidt came back up to the top of the ramp and gave me knuckles. I'm just sitting there, and before I go I always say a real quick prayer in my head. It was weird though because at the top of the ramp they're talking and introducing me and about to say for me to go, and I'm turned around, looking at Brandon. Cam's over by the side, and a bunch of friends had come up to support me, but I'm looking at Brandon, and he's, like, giving me confidence. Because you could tell that he believed I could do it. And then I did my little mental prayer thing and I was like, 'Don't let me die tonight.' Usually I'm really scared before I do a jump, but I felt, like a weird confidence because I had visualized it so much. Everything about it told my gut that it was super possible.

"The book talked about you can't even afford to think of a plan B. If you make a plan B you'll end up with plan B, so stick with plan A. So I didn't even think about what if I crashed. Sometimes I think, *Okay, if I'm going to crash I'll put my arms out just to make sure,* but this time I thought, *I'm not even going to go there. I'll figure it out if it comes to it. I'm just going to land this, stick with plan A.* And then when I was about to go in, I didn't even hesitate when they said, 'Wheelz.' I just turned around, made a quick visualization, and pushed harder than I ever have. It was weird. There was such a confidence. I felt so comforted. Usually I'm a lot more scared."

I asked Aaron, "What goes through your mind halfway down the ramp?"

He said, "You get in a tunnel vision. You're so focused. I do remember putting my hands up and throwing them forward so hard. I was really low coming into the landing before I went for the second rotation, and I even prepared myself cause I knew I

Wheelz

wasn't going to get both the rotations done real high in the air. I knew that second one would be a last-minute scary rotation. So I closed my eyes and I was like, 'Oh, please make it around.'

"When I hit my back I knew I'd underrotated it. I was overcome with happiness that I had made it to the safe part of the double flip. I mean, for the first try I almost landed it without a foam pit—without anything. I pretty much claimed it as a victory because you only really fail if you don't try. I felt like if I hadn't tried it I would have been really depressed and upset.

"Beforehand I asked some of my friends, 'What do I do if I get fired?' But I kept thinking about that book and thought, *Well, I'm chasing my dream, and as long as you're doing what makes you happy*—like, people risk stuff and it talks in this book how people risk so much to chase their dream and always pretty much come out on top. You're not just going to fail. And I thought, *Okay, if I do get fired how many people can say they got fired doing a double front flip?*

"Dov, our boss, and Cam were mad. I couldn't blame them. Their job is to keep us safe and I had gone against them. I thought they might be pleased with the attempt because it ended pretty well, but they weren't. I told them, 'Come on, I was close,' but they weren't happy.

"So I called Dov that night and told him I felt like I'm in a deadend job, like I'm not going anywhere.

And he said, 'I understand where you're coming from, but I also understand our side of it.'

It was really good to talk to him, but I told him I pretty much wanted to move on because I wanted to chase my dream. These shows *were* my dream, but I feel like maybe my dreams have changed. You always think, *Oh, this is my dream.* But sometimes you get to your dream and realize that's not your real dream. You're meant to do more.

"The next day Dov started talking about doing the double in Australia. He talked about jacking the ramp up some and what we could do to make it work. He talked about bringing in an airbag so I'd land on an airbag instead of a foam pit. But part of me is like, *I kind of want to land it without a foam pit or airbag.*"

"Before our last show I went on a safari. I figured I would hate myself if I went all the way to Africa and didn't see anything. I saw a wildebeast, an antelope, a giraffe—no lions—and a mad elephant. The elephant started coming towards us. Our driver was driving a manual transmission, so when he had to reverse away I was scared the whole time he was going to stall it and have the elephant just murder us. We were in a safari vehicle. It was open. He could have put a tusk right through us.

Wheelz

"The third show was Johannesburg. The crowd was thirty-five thousand. I went into the boss's office, and they looked at me and said, 'Do you want to do a single front flip or a double front flip?' That's when I got happy. That's when I felt like, 'Okay, they understand I want to progress. And they'll let me do it.' I felt like I'd have to throw it as hard as I could and the only way I'd be able to do that is if we adjusted the ramp a little bit."

"Before my intro, when I was just rolling to my spot, the crowd was just going nuts. I felt like Travis Pastrana. Maybe I can't compare myself to him, but it felt so cool. When they announced, 'A wheelchair athlete from Las Vegas,' and I went out and did my intro, the crowd was so loud, just applauding and stuff.

"At the top of the ramp, the crowd started going, 'Wheelz, Wheelz,' like the Wheelz chant was louder than any other night. I could feel such a good energy from the whole crowd. A lot of times the announcer will tell everyone to stand up, but this time the second they introduced me, the whole crowd just stood up. It was cool to see the whole crowd stand up because I can't. »

"When I landed the front flip, it was loud. The whole crowd was into it. They pushed me up the ramp to wave to the crowd. It was so awesome because everyone was going nuts, one of the loudest crowds."

Wheelz

Aaron described his second attempt: "From the top of the ramp, you see the motocross guys hitting the ramp on their side. It's really hectic at the top because Cam's saying, 'Go, go, go,' sending you in like paratroopers. In a situation like that you like to make sure your equipment feels good or whatever, but you're so crammed at the top there's no room to check anything. So you've got to make sure it feels good at the bottom of the ramp, and then when you get to the top and everyone's just going in, you have to go in right behind someone."

"And so when you land it you're coming in fast. You don't want to hit anyone else, but it's kind of nice too because it's so hectic you don't have time to think. If you're thinking you're probably overthinking, so it's really nice to just go."

"When I landed it all the people that had just jumped looked back. When they saw me rolling away, they were just celebrating and saying, 'Wheelz, you landed two front flips'—not two in one jump like I wanted to, but two separate front flips. I ended up getting the MVC."

"When I got MVC I was surprised because I felt like there was so much tension between me and the bosses. Telling them I wanted to retire and stuff and then having them calling me up for MVC was a really happy feeling. It felt like they kind of forgave me for being stubborn and doing what I wanted. I mean, that's *Nitro*, and none of us would have been there if we weren't stubborn and wanting to progress."

"When I went up to accept the award, they said 'the only way you can accept the award is if you let us put these giant pythons on you.' They wouldn't hand me the trophy until the snakes were wrapped around me. I couldn't even give an acceptance speech because I was freaking out."

Aaron showed me a picture on his phone and said, "You can see Dov smiling. He's got a good look on his face. It made me feel a lot better about the whole thing. I feel like he's a good person, but his job can make him really strict. Look at that smile. It was a good end."

WCMX

Aaron was invited to do a speaking tour in China. He asked me to go with him. Our best experience was seeing the transformation of Ma Yibo and his mother. I got home from China exhausted. Double jetlag in seven days is terrible. Aaron took it in stride. He was tired as well, but it is his life. He had a couple days to rest then was off to Texas.

Life Rolls On did much to promote WCMX for three years, but the competitions were always mixed with skateboarders. Texas has a competition sponsored by *RISE Adaptive Sports*. They called their event "WCMX No Excuses Throwdown." It was pure WCMX in the way Aaron always wanted it to be. He never liked being pigeonholed as a wheelchair athlete. Being raised with Am Jam suited him perfectly, but he did want WCMX to be its own sport. The competition was separated into three categories: skateboarders, BMXers, and WCMXers. Side by side they competed in their respective groups. WCMX was not this different sport competing in a corner on its own. They were as legitimate as a kid on a bike or a board.

Therefore, for the first time Wheelz competed on even ground. There were nine guys on wheelchairs in the competition. A good number of them were older than he was. Before the competition, Aaron and others coached anyone who wanted help. He told his mom he was surprised when kids would try his suggestions and they worked.

Chris Goad, Executive Director of *RISE Adaptive Sports*, wrote an article for *Sports and Spokes* about the event. The following is the article in part:

WCMX took over the Irving Convention Center at Las Colinas, Texas, for the Baylor Institute for Rehabilitation. . . . What is WCMX? Wheelchair Motocross! Haven't heard of it? You will very soon! There are no statistics showing how many currently take part in the sport, but the sense is a groundswell of popularity is bubbling under the surface primed to explode in the next few years.

> All across the country guys and girls young and old are taking their wheelchairs to skate parks to shred like any skateboarder or BMX rider. For decades there have most likely been a few thrill seekers daring enough to take to the skate park. The popularity of X-Games, more skate parks, better equipment and YouTube have created all the ingredients for WCMX to flourish. In 2006, Aaron "Wheelz" Fotheringham landed the first ever wheelchair backflip and posted it on YouTube. That video went viral with over 2 million views, and the world got its first glimpse of WCMX.

It all started for Aaron 6 years prior when he would go with his brother to the skate park. While the other kids were riding their skateboards or BMX bikes, Aaron took to the ramps on his chair. He continued to come up with new tricks and challenge himself. He then set his sights on landing the backflip, which eventually paved the way for Aaron to become an international attraction. He now travels all over the world for speaking engagements and performing with *Nitro Circus*. He's been featured in magazines, newspapers, and on television, including a Chevrolet commercial that ran during the Winter Olympics this year.

Despite all of his accolades and fame, Aaron still enjoys the simplicity of a day shredding at a skate park. He absolutely loves working with disabled kids at clinics, and is a natural at teaching and being a mentor. Kids are in awe of him, but he quickly makes them feel comfortable. Watching him during a clinic it quickly becomes apparent that he has a knack for making sure each kid gets his attention, whether it's giving pointers on doing a trick, encouraging them, or simply taking time for a photo.

Others got caught up in the WCMX fever, including current Pro Surfer and WCMX rider Christiaan "Otter" Bailey. Like Aaron, Christiaan has a passion for being a coach and mentor at WCMX clinics. He travels internationally providing clinical instruction to those hungry for the sport.

There is a whole generation of people who sustained spinal cord injuries that now are discovering WCMX. A whole other generation of kids that were born with some form of a disability are making the discovery as well. . . No longer are they feeling left out when it comes to shredding at the skate park.

Jack Harvey is a 13-year-old with spina bifida. He tried WCMX for the first time at No Excuses Throw-down. After some coaching from a couple of WCMX pros and a few unsuccessful attempts at grinding the rainbow rail, Jack made a clean run like the pros. Afterwards, Wheelz presented Jack with "Henry the lucky rock" to signify this epic achievement.

"I wanted to give this a try. I really like doing this. It's a lot of fun," said Jack. "I've been watching him (Wheelz) since I was, like, 10 years old, and he's my hero. He's given me so much inspiration and courage just to do all this stuff."

Fabian Polo, CEO of Baylor Institute for Rehabilitation of Dallas, volunteered as a participant teammate. He said, "I was blown away at the

Wheelz

athleticism of some of these competitors and the fearless attitude of the participants. It was so rewarding to see the participants be a little timid at the beginning and within 30 minutes or so they couldn't wait to get to the next obstacle. I remember vividly one young boy who was in tears for the first 10 to 15 minutes, and then see his face just light up. By the end, he was pushing himself down these very steep ramps with the biggest smile on his face. I definitely think that events like WCMX could benefit anyone in a wheelchair.

Mike Box, founder of Box Wheelchairs, never wanted to build a "skate" chair. He thought the sport was too dangerous and wanted no part of it, then came along a young Aaron Fotheringham. Mike couldn't stop Aaron from riding on his chair at the skate park, so he set out to build the safest chair possible. Each chair Aaron destroyed at the skate park led to changes and new improvements. Each Box WCMX chair is built with airplane-grade aluminum, reinforced framing, a grinding bar, adjustable rear axle compression shocks, and Frog-Legs front casters able to reach high speeds without wheel flutter. As the sport has grown so has the demand for WCMX chairs by Box, which are preferred by the top WCMX riders.

It was Wheelz and Christiaan who orchestrated the first ever adaptive skate clinic with Life Rolls On (LRO) in the summer of 2010. The summer of 2011 was another benchmark moment for WCMX. That is when WCMX was included in a competition for the first time ever. The Shoe City Open took place in Venice Beach, California, at Venice Skate Park. The formation of WCMX as an organized sport was born.

RISE Adaptive Sports continued the trend by bringing an adaptive skate clinic to Irving, Texas. RISE took these events to a whole new level when they created the concept for the No Excuses Throw-down. Building upon the adaptive skate clinics co-hosted with LRO in 2012 and 2013, RISE set out to create something all-inclusive. RISE wanted to elevate WCMX to an equal status with Skateboarding and BMX as it well deserves. No Excuses Throw-down was envisioned with the theme of "we're not looking for perfection, just No Excuses!"

Eleven-year-old Luke Acuna heard about No Excuses Throwdown a week before the event. He and his dad flew in from San Diego, California, for him to take part in the competition. Luke, who lost his leg after being hit by a garbage truck 3 years ago, was introduced to WCMX only 6 months ago. He was an avid skater with no fear prior to his injury. That same attitude has carried over to WCMX.

Wheelz

After receiving some initial instruction and technique tips from Christiaan and Wheelz on Friday, Luke was ready for the next challenge. He scaled up atop the 14-foot roll-in with volunteers assisting him with his wheelchair. Wheelz, also on top of the roll-in, gave young Luke a few pointers before he led the way down the steep ramp to a 4' 6" box jump. Luke inched forward to the edge of the ramp as the crowd began to cheer in anticipation. The crowd simmered down as he backed away from the edge and rocked his chair side to side trying to shake off the nerves.

As he again edged closer to the roll-in, the crowd noise rose simultaneously. After repeating this pattern a few more times with the crowd looking on, all eyes were on Luke as he took the plunge. He hit the box jump dead center and launched into the air, landing square on top of the ramp as the crowd erupted. He descended the box jump on the other side and was greeted by a mob of the best WCMX riders in the world. On Saturday Luke had a similar experience, dropping in for the first time from a 9-foot quarter-pipe. This time Christian demonstrated how it's to be done. With Luke 9 feet above the arena floor and his front wheels suspended in mid-air over the edge, Christiaan pointed to the exact spot he needed to land. Poised like a pro high above the crowd, he slowly rolled over the edge and nailed the landing perfectly. His

Wheelz

momentum carried him directly into the celebratory arms of Wheelz who gave him a big hug.

Baylor Institute for Rehabilitation WCMX No Excuses Throwdown presented by *RISE Adaptive Sports* was a huge success. Aaron "Wheelz" Fotheringham performed his patented flip numerous times and put on a fantastic show to take 1st place. The surprise of the competition was first-time WCMX competitor, Luke Acuna, who captured 3rd place behind Christian "Otter" Bailey's 2nd place finish. All the competitors had a great time sharing their skills and experience with the clinic participants, which was the largest group in the three years RISE has hosted.

In the weeks since WCMX No Excuses Throwdown RISE Adaptive Sports has received numerous inquiries from across the U.S. and Canada and as far away as Argentina and England about hosting a similar event in their locations. This is a testament of the interest in the sport worldwide and potential for exponential growth just beyond the horizon. Wheelchair Motocross's popularity may be bubbling under the surface now, but there are indications it may erupt on the scene in a big way very soon at a skate park near you. Stay tuned!

The next year RISE announced, "There has been an overwhelming response and space is filling up fast. WCMX

Wheelz

competitors have already registered from France, Germany, Spain, Australia, Austria, Canada, and more..."

I called Chris Goad about the competition. He said, "What I like about Aaron is he is so comfortable with all the kids. He will talk to and put his arm around the most severely disabled child as if they were old friends."

As Chris said in his article, Wheelz won the competition. The thousand-dollar prize money was nice, but what thrilled Aaron most was he won best trick. He told us the music was yanked up. He went with the rhythm and put one hand up above his shoulder with his forefinger and pinky finger up (a symbol for "rock on," though it looks like a W for Wheelz to me). At the next beat he brought his other hand up with the same signal. He pushed his wheels slightly with his elbows to start down the ramp. He rolled up another ramp, hands still frozen in place, flew into the air, and did a backflip.

I asked him, "Don't you pull on the front of your chair to get your rotation?"

He said, "I figured I could hit it by pulling back with my head and body quickly. I was right. It was a cool trick."

Shantal and Mike Box went to Texas to support him. I called Shantal to thank her for her extraordinary support. She said she

Wheelz

was amazed at the competition—that "this was truly becoming a sport."

Kumaka

A blog by Tracy Jensen about her son Kumaka gives some insight to what all this means to a child and his or her parents. Referring to her experience in Venice Beach (*Life Rolls On*), she wrote:

Dear Life,

There was a time not so long ago that being disabled was almost worse than a death sentence.

It meant living in a chair.

Watching from the sidelines.

Not included.

Not talked to.

Ignored.

Avoided.

Talked about.

Pointed at.

Laughed at.

Not taken out in public.

The wheelchairs were heavy and cumbersome.

Nothing was accessible.

It was easier to be at home.

Maybe not even easier to be home, because homes weren't accessible either.

I know that people stare at

Kumaka.

I see it.

I see kids do double takes.

I know they want to ask their parents what happened to him.

It's natural.

Parents shush their kids and pull them away.

It's happened.

Kumaka stares back.

I'm sure wishing they would come back and play.

Sometimes parents will "let" their kids come over to play.

Unless they start asking questions.

Then they gather them up.

This year something magical happened.

Kumaka was given a different kind of wheelchair.

A WCMX wheelchair.

It has changed his whole life.

There are a couple of things missing on this chair.

About twenty extra pounds.

Brakes.

Anti-tippers.

At first, he was afraid of falling.

Afraid of getting hurt.

He rolled around in this wheelchair, still living in the "wheelchair box."

Wheelz

Little by little he went faster, he pushed himself a little more.

He tried some new things.

Wheelchair basketball.

Wheelchair fun runs.

And then Venice happened.

We went to a Life Rolls On event at the Venice Skate Park.

Best Day Ever.

The event was amazing.

So many volunteers to make sure that everyone was safe.

And wonderful pros to teach everyone.

Fun with friends.

Day of smiles.

Suddenly, Kumaka has found that his chair is not a hindrance.

He's not afraid anymore.

His chair still makes him stand out.

But in a completely different way.

The chair is allowing him to LIVE.

Kids point still, and they watch him.

They want to figure out how he is balancing on two wheels.

Or how he hopped the curb.

Or how he does those 360s so fast.

They want to spin on those wheels.

Wheelz

When a toddler is learning to walk, they fall. All the time. Then they pick themselves up only to fall again. Eventually, they fall less. That's when they start walking...and then running.

When a person in a wheelchair falls, people get scared. They rush to help them. They check to make sure nothing is injured. They are told to be careful, to not hurt themselves. And of course that is all well-meaning.

But sometimes, just sometimes, people have to think outside the chair.
That's the way they only truly live.
Kumaka is learning to fall.
He's also learning how to get up.
More importantly he's learning how to keep going.
He's learning how to live and really enjoy himself doing it.

I am grateful to Mike Box, who listens to people and creates chairs that allow people to LIVE.

I am grateful to all of the coaches and athletes that have gone before Kumaka and work hard to show littles like him that there is a whole lot of fun to be had whether you are in a chair or not.

Wheelz

I am grateful for the friends we have made on this journey so far. They are near and dear to my heart. They've given my boy wings and strength to do whatever he wants to do in his life. They've taught him that the sky is the limit.

Be strong, and live beyond the chair.

I once asked Mike Box how many WCMX chairs he made. He said he sold about six WCMX chairs a month, that it was about a quarter of his business. Five months later he said, "Steve, now it's about eleven or twelve a month, about half my business."

Two weeks later he posted a picture of six WCMX frames on his shop floor with the message, "Love how fast this sport is taking off . . . This week's WCMX chair orders."

When I first inquired about those chairs, I asked, "How many of them are green?"

He said, "Most of them are green. Now and then somebody will order green. And then occasionally someone will want a green one."

I said, "Wow, that's big."

Mike responded, "You don't understand. People are seeing the possibilities of their chairs for many other things. It's not just skate parks. I'm making chairs that people use to go down

Wheelz

mountain trails. We used to make four-wheeled buggies for disabled kids to do that. Now they want it to be on their personal chairs. He's changing the world."

I was talking with some T.V. people from Brazil and bragging about Mike's chairs. One reporter told me they don't use Mike's chairs in Brazil. Their WCMXers get their chairs from a guy in Brazil. She said, "He makes strong chairs." So how big this is or how big this could get is anyone's guess.

When I called Tracy to get permission to use her blog, there was a moment when I couldn't speak. She thought we'd lost connection. I was embarrassed. But I was so moved by what all of this meant to her and her boy I just cried and couldn't get any words out.

When someone comes into my office, they won't hear about little Kumaka. I still get too emotional. The best way for me to talk about him is to write. He is not the first and he surely won't be the last to learn a wheelchair is fun. But his story is all I need.

When I regained my composure, Tracy asked if I'd seen the blog she had written months earlier. I hadn't. She sent it to me. This is it in part:

> So I started following this man [Aaron] because I knew he
> would be a great example of the "You can do anything you

Wheelz

put your mind to" mentality.

He also happens to have spina bifida.

Recently I asked Aaron to post a pic of himself wearing a green shirt to support Kumaka for his collage.

He did better.

He happened to come to California this weekend.

So he came to our house.

I KNOW!!!!!

Check out his ride. [she included a picture of Aaron's truck] Can you believe this?

AND he tricked it out with hand controls himself!

SO impressed!

A picture she included showed Aaron and Kumaka with a full 'spika' cast from his feet to his waist with a rod like a broomstick between his legs. Tracy continued,

I was so excited he put Kumaka in his trick chair. SOOO cool!

And I love that Aaron is even more amazing in person than in his videos. What a blessing to meet someone who is willing to give up some time in his schedule to hang with the boy in the giant green cast.

Love it.

Wheelz

From a mom of boys,

Tracy Jensen

Down and Discouraged

Aaron was in Brazil to be featured by T.V. Global. They had come to our home to interview Kaylene and me a couple weeks earlier for the program. He said it went well.

After the program he had a day off. He was bored, sitting in his hotel. Knowing that Bob Burnquist is from Brazil, he wrote on Bob's Instagram, "Where are you, Bob?" To Aaron's surprise Bob responded by saying he was close to his hotel. Bob came and got him and they went to a skate park. Aaron posted a picture of him and Bob and said, "Got to shred a vert pipe tonight with my friend @bobbuurnquist! And I didn't even lose my teeth this time! Still can't believe it. As a kid I always looked up to this guy and always spammed him on MySpace, and now I'm shredding alongside him! Haha, just shows that your dreams can become reality. Just keep thinking positive and working towards your goals. I have faith in all of you!"

However, by May 2014 Aaron was exhausted, alone, and depressed-anything but positive.

He had said in interviews, "I am waiting for my dreams to catch up with my reality," but in reality he had run out of dreams. He had reached all of his goals and didn't know where to go from there. His schedule had never let up since that first backflip eight years earlier.

Wheelz

For years he'd had a girlfriend named Shelly. She was a petite Peruvian, but she had a temper like Aaron's. They fought all the time and broke up a dozen times. But in May they were willing to try again.

A few days after Brazil, Aaron was headed for another Australian tour. He was not excited to go. That worried him. It worried me.

I texted him, "I saw that Texas video. You coached Jake Harvey. He said you're his hero; you inspired him and gave him courage. You gave him a rock--cool. In every town there will be a Jake Harvey. You will touch him or her and in a way say, 'I give you the gift I was born with.' Remember you're changing lives--many lives.

"Mom and I did risk a bit to adopt you, but we had been paid completely by the time you were five. Every time we hear of the Jake Harveys, we are paid again and again.

"Continue to seek out those kids. I doubt you will ever grasp how truly proud we are of you. Love, Dad."

Aaron responded, "Thank you, man. That Jake kid was awesome. I haven't seen the video yet actually! And that's a good way to look at it. That will help me be more positive, I think. Love you!!"

Wheelz

The Australian tour was much like the others. Kaylene picked him up at the airport. On the way home he told her, "*Nitro* wanted us to dress up like clowns. I told them I wasn't going to do it. I figured they'd have to fire me first before I turned my sport into a circus act. I was pretty sure they wouldn't fire me. In one of our meetings Travis stood up and said, 'This is wrong. These are professional athletes and you are disrespecting them,' and he walked out. Travis and I are the only ones that wouldn't dress up like clowns."

"Yeah, that's ridiculous. Did you get any sleep on your flight?"

"I was too tired to sleep. I think I got a few hours in. I've got one story I think you'll like."

Kaylene said, "Okay."

"It was late after our last show. I was eating pizza in the locker room by myself, wondering what I'm going to do with my life. I was tired. I was sore. I was down. Then some security guy walked into the room and asked if minded meeting with some kids. I wasn't in the mood, but I thought, *That's what I do.* So I said, 'Sure.'"

Then Aaron searched his phone and said, "Listen to this. It's from a security guard lady who was there."

Wheelz

Hi, Aaron, as promised here are a couple of photos from Saturday night. I cannot thank you enough for coming up to greet those children. When the father asked if there was a possibility that they could meet you, my first reaction was 'not a hope,' as I would like a one-dollar bill for every time I have been asked that over the last twenty-six years of working at Rod Laver.

But after looking at the smile and hope on one of the boys' faces, I thought, *What the hell*, though it is a sackable offense here to approach an artist and do a request like that. Brendan, who works the stage door, is pretty much like me, and he was the gentleman who actually told you about the kids waiting upstairs and also thought it was worth a try. We certainly did not expect you to say "Yes," but we are both extremely grateful that you did.

Such a little gesture by you in doing that has made four young boys ecstatic, although I think one of their younger sisters' reactions was the best—she screamed. I don't think you just made their night but definitely their week and almost certainly their year. They belong to a disabled sports club and I am sure their bragging rights will last the year.

Again I have been in the entertainment industry for over twenty-six years and seen many artists and performers and

Wheelz

thousands of meet-and-greets, but none compare to the spontaneous one on Saturday night.

"Stop reading," Kaylene said, wiping tears from her eyes. "I can't see the road."

Aaron read on:

"You made some of the "hard arse" security staff's eyes water by your unselfish act, not to mention all of the kids' parents too. It's the little things in life that make a difference, and you have sure made a difference to not just the boys but their families and our staff. We all left that night with the biggest smiles on our faces and massive hearts. Again, THANK YOU, you are one amazing man. I think you're a little nuts to go down that ramp though, but that's the mother in me!!!

Regards,
Debby Carter"

Aaron concluded, "That helped. What are you guys having for dinner?"

"Pulled pork sandwiches."

"Great, what time?"

"Six o'clock."

"Can Shelly come?"

"Of course."

Life Rolls On 2014

Aaron had his competition chair stolen. The local news gave him great attention. Mike Box called and said he'd have a new chair for him by the *Life Rolls On* competition. The chair was not broken in, which was a real concern for Aaron.

Joe Wickert called Kaylene for Aaron's number. She doesn't give out his number, but she sent it immediately to Joe.

A few minutes later Aaron called her: "I was so excited to hear from Joe. I kind of teared up. He offered to help in any way he could." Aaron talked about all Joe had done for him. He continued, "I want to be like Joe. He's such a good guy."

Kaylene replied, "I thought you wanted to be like Mike."

"I do."

Kaylene said, "They're both great role models. They're a lot alike."

He said, "Yeah."

Before my evening Institute class I was telling my students about all the good that had come from his chair being stolen.

A student chimed in, "I know. He's trending on Facebook."

Wheelz

I asked, "What's does trending mean?"

Instead of waiting to find his chair, Aaron drove to California with Shelly to stay with Mike Box as he made his new chair. While there he was installing a light bar on his new truck when he got a piece of metal in his eye. A doctor flushed his eye, but it was scratched. He was in extreme pain for a few days.

On our way to his competition at Venice Beach, we stopped at Mike's house. His shop is a simple garage-like shed with a table at the entrance where he sits and builds. He was working on a frame for a chair with another guy working in the back of his shop. Aaron was changing out the bearings on his new chair in a side shop.

Aaron said, "I'm feeling a bit gloomy because I can't see out of my eye."

He could barely open it. We talked for a while, but we were eager to get to the beach, so we headed for our car. Aaron and Shelly followed us. He wanted to talk, so Kaylene took Shelly aside to give us some time.

As I sat in the driver's seat with the door open, he sat in his chair facing me and said, "Shelly and I have been getting along better. We still fight a bit, but we are getting over it quicker."

Wheelz

I said, "When you see an argument coming, you need to head it off like Mom does by walking away."

He said, "That won't work with Shelly. She wants to talk it out."

I said, "You've got to find what works for you. But I'm glad you're doing better."

He said, "I'm concerned about doing a handplant in the competition because I can't see my right hand. I'm not sure I'll be able to find the coping."

I assured him he would be fine.

The morning of the competition Kaylene got a text. She said, "They found Slammy. A friend of Aaron's, Kevin Lang, found it."

We later learned that Kevin was an old skate park buddy of Aaron's. His family owns a 7-11 close to where the chair was stolen, so he knew just who to talk to. He went around with a picture of Slammy, and a kid said, "I know where it is."

He took Kevin to the house of a drug lord. Kevin had to pay the bouncer at the door forty dollars to get in. He walked past the window guy, who was apparently in charge of looking out the window, and met the boss in a back room. The boss was disabled himself and obviously too frail to have stolen the chair.

Kevin said, "I'm looking for my friend's chair." He was invited to look around. He opened a closet door and there sat Slammy. He showed the guy Slammy's picture.

The guy said, "I didn't know it was stolen. I paid seventy dollars for it. You can take it."

Kevin wheeled Slammy out, put it in his truck, and drove it to safety. Then he called Aaron, who couldn't thank him enough. Kevin became an instant hero.

One of the first people we saw when we got to Venice Beach was Evan Strong.

My wife said, "We're thrilled to see you. Congratulations on winning the gold in the Paralympics."

I said, with a smile, "I'm not thrilled to see you! You're the only one we're worried about beating our son."

He knew it was high praise, but I was a bit sincere. Whether or not Aaron was perfectly prepared for this competition, Evan could beat him, and Aaron wasn't perfectly prepared. He still

Wheelz

couldn't open his eye. I was relieved to learn from Christian Bailey that they were not pitting skateboarders against WCMXers.

As usual *Life Rolls On* held a training session for kids on wheelchairs. I was overwhelmed at the number of participants. It had more than doubled in two years. There were thirty-seven wheelchair participants in the competition and dozens of young kids on chairs, not to mention hundreds of spectators, parents, participants, and sponsors. The park was now too small. I told Christian how thrilled I was to see such a crowd.

He said, "It is this way everywhere I go internationally. You ought to see how many are doing WCMX in Australia."

Shantal, Mike Box, John Lytle, Kumuka and his mom, were there. A couple dozen two-to-eight-year-olds were there being trained by the *Life Rolls On* staff, having the time of their lives. I saw a five-year-old with a shark fin helmet, cool sunglasses, and elbow pads float expertly down a ramp on his two back wheels. His dad, wearing a shirt that read "Proud Dad" was filming him. I was so impressed with that kid—he was so cool and confident—that I went over and talked to his dad.

He said, "His name is Angelo."

I asked, "How long has Angelo been doing skate parks? He's really good."

Wheelz

"Since he was two and a half."

"Wow."

He asked who I was. At these events I love that question. I should have been wearing his shirt. I said I was Aaron's dad.

He said, "I saw Aaron do his backflip on YouTube when my wife was pregnant with Angelo. We knew he had spina bifida. Because of what I saw your son doing, I realized my son could do anything. I started checking into all the adaptive possibilities. When Angelo was two we took him to hear Aaron and his mom speak at a function called Winter Bifida. Six months later he was at a skate park. His real passion now is dance."

I thought of the book I had read twenty-two years earlier that filled me with despair. That was not this dad's experience. On the contrary he watched a kid playing on a chair and was filled with hope.

I shared with my wife what I'd just heard. She teared up and said, "Go talk to Hunter's mom." Her story about her eight-year-old was very similar. There were a couple dozen stories surrounding us, all about the same. I know it sounds weird, but I thought, *It's like they're his children.*

Before the competition began they introduced each contestant. When they announced Aaron "Aaron 'Wheelz' Fotheringham, the first to do a backflip, a double backflip, and a front flip and a *Nitro Circus* pro," he rolled up a nearby ramp and stopped by a wall of spectators separated from him by a short fence.

I thought, *What are you doing? After such an introduction you're supposed to show off a little.*

He knew that. He didn't care. There would be many opportunities that day to show off. He was taken in by a fan. She had a small pillow with his logo on it that she held up for him to see as he came up that ramp. He stopped, took the pillow out of her hands, held it next to his face, and let her take a picture. Then they talked.

When the competition began the WCMXers were to go first and Wheelz was to do the first run.

I thought that was a bad idea. "Why show the best first? Then everyone else won't look as good."

He said, "I don't know. If they know what their competition is they will know what they have to do to win."

With his helmet on and a loud crowd Aaron didn't know when his turn started. He wasted a minute of his run because no one let him know he was supposed to start. When Wheelz did his run his

Wheelz

eye took more of a toll on him than he realized. He could see good enough to do his tricks, but the stress of not seeing in one eye and the worry about having to use a new chair had worn him out. His run lacked the energy I'd seen two years earlier. Nevertheless he landed his tricks. He ran horizontally with his chair splitting the coping, his upper wheels about two feet in the air. He landed his handplant a few times. His run was short, but fine.

Aaron was disappointed. When the skateboarders got their turns, Evan did a great job. He ground the top of the coping that Aaron had split, then turned down for a cool run. He had told us he wasn't there to compete with Aaron. He just wanted to land the trick he was working on. He landed it and it was good. All I could think was, *Thank heavens they're not competing against each other.*

After the individual runs they had a jam session. Anyone who wanted could take a turn. Wheelz now had something to prove-- that his run wasn't him. He went hard and fast. He did spins and drop-ins on the ramps that were just cool. He had two guys push him to do his backflip and did that horizontal run along the top of the bowl with his hands on his helmet.

After the jam session, a bunch of WCMXers went up a ramp onto a grinding bar. Many struggled and fell off the side. The crowd appreciated every attempt. If nothing else it proved wheelchairers are not fragile. Aaron did the bar with ease. Frankly, it was nothing compared to the rainbow grind.

Then he did something that for me was the trick of the day: He went hard and fast up that ramp at an angle. That shot him over the grinding bar and landed him on a down ramp on the other side of it. It surprised everybody.

When the judges announced the winners Evan won "Best Overall Run" for skateboarders. David Lebuser won "Best Overall Run" for WCMXers.

David and Aaron are good friends. David "is the first professional wheelchair skater in Germany."[viii] After he broke his back, while still in the hospital, a friend showed him a video of Aaron doing a backflip, "which inspired him to go to skate parks and start wheelchair skating."[ix] David hosts WCMX workshops for other wheelchair users in Germany.

Wheelz, for his backflip, won best trick. Taking home one of the three first place checks ($500 each), he did not feel like he lost. He felt great about the day and was thrilled for David's win.

Kaylene and I ended the day being interviewed by ESPN. They were doing a documentary on Aaron and Travis.

They asked, "What do you see in Aaron's future?"

Wheelz

It is a question Kaylene and I have discussed often. We have our concerns. But I often consider what William James, a psychologist and philosopher, once wrote:

> True genius is the ability to see things in an un-habitual way. It is the greatest gift one human being can give another, the very essence of freedom, because in seeing things differently and sharing that new view one opens up more space for communion, for confidence, and for love."[x]

It was Angelo's confidence I kept thinking about. His father's hope had touched our hearts. He'd seen things in an un-habitual way. That our son had a part in that, well, there are no words to describe how we felt. And so I responded, "I'm fully aware of what happens to childhood stars when the lights go down and the cameras go away. When he comes down to reality, it may be very hard on him. Or he may go on to a great speaking career. Either way nothing can ever take away from him the lives he has changed."

At the end of April 2015, Wheelz won the WCMX World Championship in Texas. There were about sixty kids who came to be trained and about twenty who came to compete. *RISE Adaptive Sports* has taken the batton and will ensure WCMX lives on. Aaron was scared. He wasn't sure he would win. But on the ride home from the airport, he told his mom, "They all do cool tricks, but they only do a couple. I do many."

Wheelz grew up in the BMX world, where a trick or two won't win any competitions. He still goes to Woodward and the skate parks whenever he gets a chance. He still loves to learn new tricks and make viedeos out of new material. Last week he rolled off a house onto a ramp. I can't imagine him ever letting up.

Conclusion

"Live your life on the edge of your seat." Aaron Fotheringham

This book isn't about turning lemons into lemonade. It's about liking lemons. When Aaron told Greg Haerr, "It sucks for you that you have to walk," I knew at that moment I had to tell this story. I wanted the world to know this wasn't a kid coming up with a clever line to cope with a disability. That was Aaron to the core.

Aaron would later say, "When life gives you a wheelchair, find a skate park."

He means that. He did that.

We have a picture of Aaron when he was three. He was part way into a field trying to follow Brian and Lisa. His mom had told him he couldn't go because they were heading to climb a mountain. That made him mad, so he headed off into the field to follow them anyway.

My wife thought he was so cute—angry—determined, so she took the picture. It shows him making his own path. That is telling. But the value of the picture is that it shows those two tip casters turned up.

Wheelz

Only by doing that could he get his front wheels off the ground. Only by doing that could he make that path his path. The only thing disabled on that chair was those casters. What Aaron offers the world is that attitude, and the cool thing is that attitude is contagious.

There are millions of individuals with serious challenges who succeed in spite of them. They inspire us. That's not Aaron. He is among those who find joy in the challenge itself. He is not successful in spite of it; he is successful because of it.

He was once sitting at McDonald's when a preacher came up to him and told him after this life he would walk. He knew the guy meant well, but that irritated him. He said to me, "What makes him so sure I will want to?"

We have a new wing at the Las Vegas airport. The floor is like smooth marble. Once, Aaron had to check each carousel to find his luggage. No one was around. The distance was about 200 feet. He flew across that floor as fast as a kid on a bike. I didn't even try to keep up with him. He floated so quietly on that floor I was jealous. Telling him "Someday you will walk" is like telling me "Someday you'll wear shackles around your ankles."

Everyone he comes in contact with catches that attitude. And the neat thing is he's coming in contact with millions. Everywhere he goes he's interviewed by local news stations. They show him at

Wheelz

stake parks, with *Nitro*, or just spinning on flat ground. They show him enjoying life. With that kind of exposure, that attitude could go viral.

As much as I want the world to know who Aaron really is, I think there is something more. I keep thinking about John Lytle's cartoons. Did they somehow prepare the way for some to accept Aaron, or were they just a cool coincidence? I know they prepared John to be a significant contributor in his life.

I also think of John and Mike Box. Without them the possibility of Aaron being Wheelz seems remote. I also think of those skate parks Joe Wickert built.

When we were first married and living in Las Vegas, we visited my wife's brother Frank a couple times. He had just built a house out in the northwest part of the valley. We thought he was crazy to build so far away from the city. He was surrounded by desert.

My wife's parents loaned Frank the money to build the house. Years later, when we were living in Tucson, they came to visit us. They told us Frank was letting the house go into foreclosure. He was letting their retirement savings go to the bank.

While they were visiting us, Kaylene had a dream one night. She dreamed we split that house into two houses and were living in it together. She told her father of the dream. We offered to save the house with the equity from our house, add on to it, and move in together.

Her father's reaction seemed strange to us: "I always wanted someone to take care of my wife when I'm gone."

It was strange because she had heart problems and he was in perfect health. The odds of her outliving him seemed remote. We moved to Vegas and started renovating the home. We were not there more than a month when my wife's father was killed in a car accident.

The family was devastated, but they were also grateful Kaylene's mom was not left alone. As of this writing, twenty-five years later, she is still alive and well.

We liked living out in the empty desert. When the city grew in our direction, we liked the conveniences that offered as well. And when the skate parks came we figured that was nice. It gave Brian something to do.

With hindsight it seems more than a coincidence that we ended up living in the most optimum place on earth for Aaron to grow up. I doubt there are many homes on the planet that are within easy rolling distance to four skate parks.

In Malcolm Gladwell's book *Outliers*, an outlier is someone who stands out from the norm. The book makes a big deal out of timing and favorable circumstances. If you're going to be a hockey pro, you need to be born in January, February, or March in Canada. The timing of Canadian league play gives early births an advantage. The book gives several individual examples, like Bill Gates being born at the right time and the right place to make his contribution to computers.

Outliers points out it's good to be gifted, and circumstances (good or bad) have their helping role. But if you don't work hard, you won't be an outlier. They figure outliers generally put in at least 10,000 hours in their chosen field. My son is an outlier. His gift we've discussed. His favorable circumstances I've mentioned. He has put in way more than 10,000 hours. I've done the math.

My question is, who is the timing for – Aaron "Wheelz" Fotheringham, Kumaka Jensen, Zachary Pudy, or someone who hears this story? Indeed, who couldn't benefit from seeing their challenges as advantages? But if I've learned anything from Aaron, it's that it's not our challenges that define us; it's our gifts.

I believe everyone has been given a gift. I believe we have been placed in a time and a place to magnify those gifts. I assume many people believe the same. Paul said as much in the New Testament (see Acts 17:26). In the Old Testament, Deuteronomy 32:8 and the story of Esther (see Esther 4:14) offer the same idea.

Wheelz

I believe the person that finds his or her gift and puts in the time will change the world. I know a lady who cried for years because she couldn't bear children, but she had a gift of wanting unwanted children. She still cries, but now it is for kids in China who glimpsed a possibility. It's a "good cry."

As we put in the hours, I suggest we remove any tip casters, wear a helmet and enjoy the ride.

THE END

VIDEO 9: This last video (Aaron "Wheelz" Fotheringham – The Story) is one of the best:

http://goo.gl/iiAx0i

About the Author

Steve Fotheringham has a Bachelor's Degree in Psychology from Weber State University, A Master's Degree in Marriage and Family Counseling, and a Doctorate Degree in Educational Administration from The University of Arizona. But the only credentials he claims for this book is that he was an eyewitness.

With family and news videos, text messages, emails, Aaron's written stories, journal entries, magazine and news articles, and DVR recordings that cover much of his life, coupled with the fact that Steve and his wife Kaylene were there most of the time, he was able to write an accurate biography.

Editor

Shaunna Sanders has a Bachelor's Degree from Southern Utah University and a Master's Degree from the University of Nevada, Las Vegas, both of which are in English Literature. She is a novelist and a mother of four.

[i] Cover by Marcelo Sayao , rights purchased from Corbis, August 21, 2013, Andrew.gutterson@corbis.com or Sales.LA@corbis.com;

[ii] (All I Ask of You – music by Andrew Lloyd Webber, lyrics by Charles Hart and Richard Stilgoe). © copyright 1986 The Really Useful Group Ltd., London. All Rights Reserved. Used by permission of the copyright owner.

[iii] (Attributed to Abraham Lincoln, found in a speech by Robert R. Steuer, Brigham Young University, September 30, 2008).

[iv] (Neal A. Maxwell, April 2000, LDS General Conference).

[v] Ellen Stohl (Disabled Dealer Magazine, October 2009).

[vi] (online.wsj.com/article/SB124381163117170381.html)

[vii] (Desert Saints Magazine, p. 12-14, October 2010)

[viii] Wikipedia biography on David Lebuser.

[ix] Wikipedia biography on David Lebuser.

[x] (Hiott, Andrea, Thinking Small, The Long Strange Trip of the Volkswagen Beetle, Hiott, Ballantine Books, New York, 2012. This book quotes William James, p. 373).

CPSIA information can be obtained
at www.ICGtesting.com
Printed in the USA
FSHW020812041118
53541FS